Speaking Up®

Surviving Executive Presentations

Speaking Up®

Surviving Executive Presentations

Frederick Gilbert

PowerSpeaking, Inc.
Redwood City, CA

Speaking Up®: Surviving Executive Presentations

Frederick Gilbert

Published by: PowerSpeaking, Inc.
200 B Twin Dolphin Drive
Redwood City, CA 94065
Info@powerspeaking.com
650-631-8459

Cover design: Lamirande Design
Interior design: Robaire Ream

ISBN 978-0-615-58338-9

Printed in U.S.A. by Andover Printing, South San Francisco, CA

First U.S. Edition: March, 2012

For Mary McGlynn whose belief in this project and in me has made it all possible.

Table of Contents

FIGURES

TABLES

Acknowledgements

"It takes a village," is a cliché that describes the evolution of this book perfectly. Although I am the author of the book, there have been literally hundreds of people without whose help this project could not have come to life.

The executives who have been so generous with their time and so willing to share their expertise are at the center of this work. I am very grateful to them. A special thanks goes to the eleven people who opened their hearts and minds to make Part IV possible: Dan Warmenhoven, Felicia Marcus, Ginger Graham, Dan Eilers, Anna Eshoo, Ned Barnholt, John Kispert, Audrey MacLean, Steve Blank, Brenda Rhodes, and Rick Wallace. They talked about their backgrounds, mentors, families, and legacies. Their shared passions and insights will make the next generation more successful.

I have referred to the six mid-level managers who volunteered to present in front of the C-levels as our "heroes." Reflecting the highest levels of professionalism that have made their careers so successful, they showed up with actual presentations from their corporate "day jobs." For teaching purposes, they presented ineffectively and took the punches from the executives like good sports. Then applying the strategies at the heart of *Speaking Up*®, they came back for a second presentation and were successful. Thank you for being so creative, improvisational, and a pleasure to work with: Todd Lutwak, Julie Patel, Andy Billings, Sharon Black, Randi Feigin, and Brent Bloom. This book would not exist without you.

We have been developing and researching these concepts for 10 years. Along the way valuable stories, data, and insights have been provided by the roughly 10,000 mid-level people who have taken this training. It was sometimes poignant:

"I'm becoming a real asshole"; it was sometimes angry: "They (senior management) get to tell stories, but we don't"; and it was sometimes funny: Bob Drolet's suggestion, "You might as well find out what the rub is. Why waste twenty more minutes? Take the bullet now." All that input has made our *Speaking Up*® training program, and this book, more accurate and realistic. I deeply appreciate people's willingness to share their experiences at the top level.

Speaking of top level, our team of world-class trainers at PowerSpeaking, Inc. has been central to the development of this book. Over the years their insights about this topic and their classroom "war stories" have helped to fine-tune this content. While all of this was happening, David Azevedo kept PowerSpeaking, Inc. humming along, and Moira Kavanaugh provided valuable insights and unflagging enthusiasm for the project. I am especially grateful to Melissa Schwartz who has lived and breathed this program alongside me for many years.

Turns out that writing a book isn't as simple as I thought. It is one thing to sit typing away week after week, month after month. It is quite another to get the story right and to get the flow to work for the reader. Then there's text editing. Then there's layout and design. So before this book went to press, about a dozen people had a hand in shaping the final product. Their input made it so much better. For their help with content, I want to thank Nina Solomita and Linden Gross. Joel Rutledge did an amazing job of transcribing the hours of taped interviews. Mark Lamirande was always there quickly responding to my picky concerns about the graphics.

Five years before the book got started, we launched a video project that brought all this to life: *Speaking to the Big Dogs*®. On that project, as well as on our follow-up program *Speaking Up*®: *Presenting to Executives*, I have been fortunate to have worked with the world's greatest video producer, Greg Bezat. His directing, editing, and post-production work was done with great finesse and good humor. I also want to thank Bill Bishop who was hugely helpful in the video production. Photographers Mark Hatasaka and Paul Grant supplied me with the stills that populate this book. I am deeply grateful for their skills. Patricia Hamilton was so helpful with the early stages of layout and Robaire Ream did the final design.

Michael Sizemore and Lisa Rothman were superb text editors who fixed things I didn't see even after reading it for the tenth time. All of this made me appreciate that when a big New York firm publishes your book, you get the benefit of a tall office building filled with English majors who do all of this for you. Hmmm, maybe next time?

Bob Dreher

Sadly, two of the people who were most critical to my development as a psychologist, Bob Dreher and Bob Suzcek, are no longer around to hear my appreciation. They were professors at San Francisco State University who opened up the world of social science research to me as a "young dog." At Saybrook University I refined my thinking about such issues and developed my confidence to jump into big questions like this book addresses when I did my PhD dissertation, *Jazz, Rock and Roll, and the Revolution in*

Rick, 1973

Psychotherapy. Speaking Up® would not have happened without all this encouragement early on in my career. As Steve Jobs reminded us in his famous 2005 Stanford commencement speech, you can only connect the dots looking backwards.

Fred Gilbert

While the focus of this book is the past ten years, the spark for it all started when I was in junior high and high school. I loved speaking to groups and being "on stage" for whatever reason. I see now my father's influence in all of this. He was an executive for a large insurance company in San Francisco. He took a number of night school courses in public speaking. He used to encourage me, "People who can get up and speak well are going to be leaders.

You should work on it." How right he was. Who knew it would turn into a business, a career, and a book?

Mary McGlynn

Finally, I have dedicated this book to my wife and partner, Mary McGlynn. Her unerring sense of what hits the mark and what misses it has made this book incalculably better. She and I developed the initial questions about presenting at the top level in 2001 and worked together hammering out the basic concepts and approach to this research. Mary has been there for me from the initial phases to the final edits. She didn't complain when evenings and weekends went by with me staring at a computer screen. I am so appreciative of her support.

It truly does "take a village," and I've been fortunate to have great people in my village. Thank you all.

—Rick Gilbert

Preface

"For middle management, our quarterly board meetings are terrifying events. Every three months this hallway is lined with people in black suits with their presentations clutched in their hands and panic in their eyes," said our tour guide at the Atlanta, Georgia world headquarters of the Coca-Cola Company. She added, "The tension is so high, I stay away from here on those days."

If you are in middle management, you live with daily ambiguity, lack of control, and even chaos. To get anything done, you must present your ideas to people up the chain, and those presentations can be brutal. Careers and projects can come unwound in a matter of minutes if the presenter doesn't know the rules at the top level. Your people depend on you being successful so that you will "bring home the bacon." Although you may be confident speaking at your own level, as you go up the organization, your confidence can crumble knowing that the stakes are higher, and at the same time, the rules are very different from day-to-day presentations. What *are* these rules? That is what this book is about.

The good news is, the rules are simple and easy to learn: 1) know the people; 2) get to the point; and 3) improvise. Unfortunately a staggeringly high number of mid-level people (67%, actually) march right into top-level meetings and shoot themselves in the foot by: 1) not saying what they want at the beginning; 2) having too many PowerPoint slides; and 3) rigidly sticking to their scripts. This is a formula for career suicide.

We've researched this topic for the past ten years, interviewing C-level executives, and getting input from literally hundreds of mid-level managers. The strategies you will learn in this book come directly from the executives who tell you exactly what to do to be successful in those high stakes meetings. In addition, this material has been "road tested" in hundreds of classes. We get feedback constantly from graduates who tell us stories of deals won and careers enhanced when they applied the principles you are about to learn.

We teach classes on this topic, both live and web-based. We also offer an award winning (Brandon Hall Gold Excellence in Learning) in-depth, on-demand, self-paced course called *Speaking Up®: Presenting to Executives* that streams to your computer. This book is interconnected with that video program. On the last page of some of the chapters you will notice a QR tag. If your smartphone or tablet has a QR tag scanning app, you can go right to the videos that are the foundation of our *Speaking Up®* online program. Some we've found that work well are: i-nigma (http://itunes.apple.com/us/app/i-nigma-qr-code-data-matrix/id388923203?mt=8) and Microsoft tag (http://tag.microsoft.com/download.aspx). There are lots of other free QR tag readers. Find the one that works best with your device.

For more information about our programs, please visit our web page: www.powerspeaking.com.

Finally, as this book is going to press, the European and United States' debt crises promise to make our economic future uncertain at best, and catastrophic at worst. This book is about the skills that C-level executives told us will keep careers on track because they help their corporations be more competitive. Obviously, *Speaking Up®* communication skills are not the be all and end all of a successful career, but having them will surely be a success factor as you keep your boat afloat in the choppy waters ahead.

I hope you enjoy this book and find it helpful.

Rick Gilbert
rick@powerspeaking.com
1-650-631-8459

Introduction

I started PowerSpeaking, Inc. in 1985 to teach people how to make winning, career-building business presentations with confidence. Because the demand for these skills is huge, our company has been very successful. Our trainings provide excellent tools for people who present to their own departments, to subordinates, and to peers. By the early 2000s, however, I started hearing horror stories from mid-level managers about the terror they felt when presenting to senior-level management. Top-level meetings clearly require a different approach. One of our clients learned this lesson the hard way when he had a complete meltdown at a C-level meeting.

No Stories! Fire Gilbert!

Matt was a *PowerSpeaking*® graduate and a vice president of IT at a $3 billion Silicon Valley company. Preparing for a presentation to the founders and top officers of his company, he came to me for one-on-one presentation coaching. I drilled him on the importance of using stories to connect with his audience and to create long term retention of his core message. The research is crystal clear that stories are more powerful than data in this regard.[1]

In his own departmental meetings, Matt had used storytelling successfully. A major problem occurred, though, when, following my advice, he tried the same approach in his quarterly presentation to the executive staff. A few minutes into Matt's story to illustrate one of his key points, the COO bellowed, "Where the hell are you going with this? Get to the point!"

Matt's response reverted to childhood and made matters worse. Looking plaintively at the COO, he stammered, "Well, Rick Gilbert, the presentation coach you sent me to, told me to use stories." Matt seemed to be looking for approval from a stern father. But instead of approval, the COO yelled, "Well, fire Gilbert and get on with it." It was a bad day for Matt and a bad day for me.

As the speech coach who had just been fired, I called the COO to find out what had gone wrong. I told him about the research showing that stories move people more than data, and that stories aid in retention. I will never forget his blunt response, "We don't have time for stories, and I don't care about retention. We have to get the next agenda item on the table, make a decision, then move on."

Suddenly a light bulb went on above my head. It was instantly clear that what works in most presentation situations can cost you your job in higher-level meetings. That conversation with the COO literally changed our business from that day to this.

Different Rules at the Top

Since that eye-opening exchange with Matt's COO, we have been studying the dynamics of senior-level meetings. Like cultural anthropologists, we set out to explore the unique set of rules in this strange land referred to as "the C-suite." We asked questions, such as: How can major projects and success-ful careers fall apart in a matter of moments at a senior meet-ing? Conversely, how does one become a corporate hero in the C-level meeting room?

To find the answers, we conducted in-depth, video-based interviews with 22 C-level executives. They shared priceless insights about how to survive and even thrive in the often brutal life at the top levels of corporate America. What they revealed, although not exactly secret, is generally unknown in the lower ranks. This explains why so many mid-level managers fail when presenting to C-level executives.

Abaca CEO Steve Kirsch being interviewed

In short, the insights these high-ranking executives shared will help you avoid presentation pitfalls and boost your professional standing in the process. Now let's meet our senior executives.

Greg Ballard
SVP, Warner Brothers

Ned Barnholt
Chairman, KLA-Tencor

Steve Blank
Founder, Former CEO, Epiphany

Robert Drolet
Brig. General (Retired), Former Defense Industry Executive

Dan Eilers
General Partner, Vanguard Ventures, Former CEO, Claris Corporation

Doris Engibous
Board Member, Natus Corporation, Former CEO, Hemosphere, Inc.

Anna Eshoo
Member, U.S. Congress California's 14th District

Harold Fethe
VP, Anacor Pharmaceuticals

Ginger Graham
Board Member, Walgreens, Former CEO, Amylin Pharmaceuticals

Vern Kelley
SVP, Intersil Corporation

Steve Kirsch
CEO, Abaca

John Kispert
CEO, Spansion, Inc.

Introduction

Bryan Lamkin
CEO, Clover Network,
Former SVP, Yahoo, Inc.

Mark Leslie
Founder, Former CEO,
Veritas Software

Mike Lyons
Venture Partner, Paladin
Group, Associate Professor,
Stanford University

Audrey MacLean
Co-Founder, NET, Former
CEO, Adaptive, Associate
Professor, Stanford
University

Felicia Marcus
Western Director, Natural
Resources Defense
Council, Former Regional
Administrator, EPA

Corinne Nevinny
General Partner,
LMNVC

Brenda Rhodes
Chairman and CEO,
InTouch Communications

Jane Shaw
Chairman, Intel

Rick Wallace
CEO, KLA-Tencor

Dan Warmenhoven
Executive Chairman,
NetApp

Knowing what the expectations are at the top can mean the difference between a successful career and a new job search. Unfortunately, these lessons aren't taught in business schools, but are often learned via real life fiascos. Throughout this book, you will hear directly from these C-level executives. They will tell you the best ways to present to them. Their advice can literally save your career, get your project funded, or even help your company pull ahead of the competition. In the following pages, you will get all the information you need to survive the rough and tumble of a senior-level meeting.

Speaking Up®: Surviving Executive Presentations is divided into four parts. Each part explores a different element of engaging with top-level decision makers. Whether you work in a corporate setting or a nonprofit environment, the communication issues you face are the same.

In Part I, we look in depth at who the C-levels really are. In Part II, we review the major problems—the "Seven Deadly Challenges"—that can derail your well-prepared presentations. You will follow the plights of six mid-level executives as they learn some hard lessons on the playing fields of "Mahogany Row." In Part III, we provide a presentation plan that will keep your executives paying attention to you instead of their smartphones. In Part IV, the executives let you into their world on a personal level. The greater your understanding of who they really are, the quicker you will be able to create a collaborative relationship with them when you step up to the table and say, "Good morning." Finally, on pages 185–188 there is a glossary of terms used throughout this book.

Let's get started . . .

PART

I

The People at the Top

Having worked as a psychologist, consultant, and college teacher, I had zero idea about management structure or strategy when I joined Hewlett-Packard in 1980. As you'll see in Chapter 1, I found out the hard way that what you don't know *can* hurt you. The lessons I learned over the years (mostly about what not to do) became rich background for this book. After reading *Speaking Up®: Surviving Executive Presentations*, you won't have to make the same mistakes I made.

In the famous military treatise, *The Art of War*, Sun Tzu advises, "Know your enemy and know yourself, and you can win a hundred battles without a single loss."[1] In Chapter 2, you will meet your "enemy." While life at the top levels of corporate America can be very competitive and feel like a battlefield sometimes, the executives sitting around that table are not your enemy. Thus, the war metaphor is limited. In fact they see you as a colleague. As Dan Warmenhoven reminded us, "We're all on the same team. We're all in the same company. We are all pursuing the same objectives."

Of course, the more you know about your "colleagues" before walking into that room, the better. Chapter 2 takes you behind the glossy annual reports, to reveal what life is like for people at the C-level: their lack of job security, the competitive nature of their jobs, and the journeys they've taken to get where they are. Understanding all this, plus the skills you are going to learn in the rest of this book, will allow you to win your boardroom "battles."

CHAPTER

1

Clueless

A presentation cannot make a career, but a presentation can undo a career.

—Bryan Lamkin

As a mid-level manager, you are accustomed to leading your own meetings. You may be a very successful leader with 30 or 300 people under you. In your quarterly off-site meetings with your entire team, your presentations are enthusiastically received. You are a respected and successful leader. Your career is on track. The problem is, when you walk into those quarterly review meetings with the C-level staff, all bets are off.

The stakes could not be higher. Your job, your project, and the jobs of those people who report to you hang in the balance every time you get up to present to senior leadership. This is make or break time. Many a boardroom has been bloodied by the carnage left in the wake of an unprepared speaker, clueless about the rules of the game. It happened to me.

How I Went Down in Flames

I confidently walked into Dick Anderson's spacious office at the Hewlett-Packard Computer Systems Division in Cupertino, California. I was manager of our quality publications and training programs. The year was 1982 and I was just two years into my business career. It was my first meeting with a real senior executive. I was accompanied by my boss, Ilene Birkwood, the functional manager of Quality Assurance, who reported to Dick, the general manager of the division of 3,000 people. Our meeting had been scheduled for 30 minutes, but ended abruptly in 15. We didn't get what we wanted. In spite of my

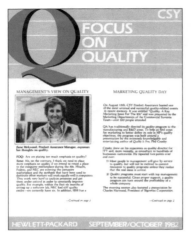

Focus on Quality

confidence, something had gone terribly wrong, and I didn't know what it was, or why it happened.

With the clarity of 20/20 hindsight and years of research, I now see what went wrong at that meeting. First of all, I presumed that this meeting was all about me, and a big deal in Dick Anderson's day. After all, I was a manager, and what could be more important than my quality training program? Well, a whole lot, actually. Although huge for me, my presentation was only a small part of Dick's complicated schedule that day.

Dick Anderson had much bigger, more compelling concerns than me or my proposal. He had just made national business headlines. During the early 1980s, the Japanese were making inroads not only into the automotive industry, but also into the world of high-tech. Their attack on American commerce dominated the business and popular press. In this competitive environment, Dick had made the decision to buy Japanese-made computer components because of their proven higher quality. As Dick said at the time, "We want to build high quality computers, but how can we do that if the memory chips keep failing?"

Newsweek, Aug 9, 1982

This had created quite an uproar and brought him attention from HP corporate offices. His focus that day might have been on a few other things—perhaps an interview with *Business Week* in the next half-hour or pos-

At a forum in Washington D.C., Dick Anderson had made a speech focusing on the stunning difference in quality between Japanese and American vendors of integrated circuits. American vendors, notably, Intel, were at first enraged, then sheepishly apologetic, and then energized into reaction and repair.[1]

—Chuck House and Ray Price
The HP Phenomenon

sibly his upcoming meeting with the HP Board. Dick oversaw an entire division of HP. His interest in my little slice of the pie was, to say the least, limited. *(See Dick's reflections on our meeting in the summary of Part I, page 29.)*

Your presentation is vitally important to you, but remember the executives are processing information from 25 to 50 different parts of the company.

—Felicia Marcus

The biggest lesson I teach executives and students is that your worldview is pretty narrow. The people above you are dealing with a much larger context than you are, and if you want to get good quickly, you need to understand more than your little piece.

—Steve Blank

The second mistake I made was seeing Dick as a father figure who would give me a pat on the back for my brilliant training efforts. With a background in humanistic psychology, I had hoped we could create a bond through our mutual commitment to training and the human potential. After all, aren't happy, fulfilled, even self-actualized employees good for business? Couldn't our quality training programs create peak experiences for them? Surely Dick would want to work with me toward the lofty goal of enriching his employees' work experiences.

Well, not exactly.

Yes, Dick had set aside a half hour in his demanding schedule for our meeting, but it was my responsibility to let him know why we were there and what we needed from him. It was up to Ilene and me to get that message across clearly and quickly, then get the hell out of his office. As soon as he became aware that we didn't have our act together, the meeting was over. He knew enough to value his time even if we didn't.

Since I made that ineffective presentation to Dick Anderson, the senior-meeting challenge is more treacherous than ever for mid-level managers. With growing pressure from issues like globalization and the speed of business on the Internet, performance demands on senior leadership increase daily. There's no time for, "Hi Bob. How was your weekend? How's the family?" Today's demand is: "Let's get right to it. I have another meeting in ten minutes."

I walked into that meeting like a naïve schoolboy hoping to please his teacher, rather than an effective professional. I lacked the knowledge of HP's overall objectives, or Dick's objectives, or how my department could support those objectives. To put it mildly, I was clueless.

Summary

Our company has worked with thousands of mid-level managers and executives preparing them to "speak up." I can assure you that what happened to me as I struggled to understand how to relate to senior leadership is not uncommon. If you enter corporate life without formal business training, as I did, you will learn these communication rules by trial and error, if at all. It doesn't need to be that way. What follows is a road map, a compass, and a GPS to help guide you on your journey into that unknown territory called "the C-suite." These are the tools that will help you be successful every time you "speak up" in your organization.

Now let's learn more about the people sitting around that big table who are waiting for your opening line.

2

Life at the Top

*Executives are paid to be paranoid. Executives
are territorial. Executives are impatient.*
—Harold Fethe

Your success depends on getting through to C-level executives on their terms. Let's be clear about this—presenting to C-levels (or other senior decision makers in your company) will simply be the most important presentations you will ever make in your entire life. Ever! In your entire life! Think about it. You probably will not go into politics or entertainment where you could be in front of huge audiences at say, the Democratic or Republican national conventions, or on the steps of the Lincoln Memorial speaking to hundreds of thousands of people. Nope. Probably not going to happen.

More likely

Yet your 45-minute presentation in the boardroom in front of a dozen people who are not there to be entertained or inspired could get your project approved, could get you promoted, and could make you a hero to your family and your team . . . or not.

The toughest audience you will ever face are high IQ, high self-esteem males. The research also shows that high IQ, high self-esteem females are only slightly more forgiving.[1] Welcome to C-level land.

Input from C-level executives makes it clear that their expectations are unique. The rules are different at the top, and are often a mystery to mid-level managers. Understanding executives at the top level—their personalities, the stresses of their positions, what they demand from mid-level managers— is key to successful communication in and out of the meeting room. Conversely, not understanding whom you're dealing with can be career suicide.

> If you don't have that one element—the ability to communicate, the ability to present, the ability to persuade—then you're not going to go to the higher echelons of that organization. You're just not going to make it.
>
> —Robert Drolet

People who get to the top have traits that set them apart. They are extremely bright, aggressive, successful Type 'A' personalities. Most are males and often Ivy League educated. They are under heavy pressure to produce in a highly competitive environment. Your goals must be in line with their goals: to move the company forward. They don't have time for pleasantries, diversions, or people who can't respond quickly to their demands. Here we'll look at the reality that defines their world.

Warning: this is not a pleasant stroll in the park, and it is occasionally 'R' rated.

Alpha Personality "Syndrome"

Life for people at the top levels of corporate America is a competitive, power-driven, dog-eat-dog world. And they know it. Witness Chuck Tyler, physics PhD, who headed up a major Hewlett-Packard research lab back in the early 1980s. With 100 engineers and scientists under him, he proudly quipped to me one day, "I'm the intellectually dominant primate in the room."

In our research on the personalities of top-level executives, we did a survey of middle management to see how they perceived people at the top. For a period of six months in our training workshops, we had people describe the personalities and business values of their C-level executives. Content analysis of the surveys showed that the top five adjectives used to describe senior leaders were: *data-driven, impatient, aggressive, time-pressured, and intimidating.* Perhaps these are qualities that boards prize in CEOs, but they probably don't describe someone you'd like to have over for dinner.

It may be a stretch to say there is an "alpha male" or "alpha female" personality syndrome simply because there is such a wide variety of successful styles among top-level executives. Consider the huge differences between well-known CEOs: Bill Hewlett and Dave Packard (*The HP Way*); Andy Grove at Intel (*Only the Paranoid Survive*); Larry Ellison at Oracle ("We eat our young."); Bill Gates at Microsoft; Steve Jobs at Apple. Yet, it is undeniable that there are commonalities among people at the top. Their idiosyncrasies help to build the companies they founded, but they can also cause pain to people who work for them.

Writing in the *New York Times*[2] on the death of George Steinbrenner, Benedict Carey commented, "Recent research on status and power suggests that brashness, entitlement,

Alphas Run Companies

In reviewing a study of alpha baboons, the *Wall Street Journal*[3] commented, "In the human savannah, where smarts matter more than brute strength, alphas run companies, amass fortunes, and dominate any meeting they're in. They are ambitious, assertive, confident, and competitive."

and ego are essential components for any competent leader." Psychologist Kate Ludeman noted in the *Harvard Business Review*[4], "Possessing both intimidating personalities and genuine power, alphas expect the world to show them appropriate deference." According to Andrew Park in *Fast Company*[5] magazine, "Convinced of their greatness, these alpha males lapse into arrogance, defensiveness, manipulation, and malevolence, leaving a tangle of confusion and unhappiness."

Why are these descriptors so harsh? Performance pressure, for one thing. CEOs answer to many audiences: shareholders, analysts, employees, customers, management, even community groups. One minute they're dealing with a Wall Street phone call, and the next minute they're making an employee video. As we'll see in Part IV, they describe living in a kind of fishbowl. Ginger Graham confided that she can't have a bad day and be wearing a frown, or forget someone's name for fear of sending the wrong message. And that's just the start of the pressure.

What Job Security?

Why is it a bare knuckles world at the top level? For starters, there isn't much job security. If you plan to work with C-levels to get things done, be advised they won't be there for long. According to *CLO*[6] magazine, the average tenure for someone in the "C-suite" is only 23 months.

These statistics are confirmed by Karen Sage, VP Marketing, CA Technologies:

> Tenuous job security doesn't impact just the CEO, but all upper executive-level staff. It's about holding leadership accountable. Someone has to take the fall. Another situation to note is that most leaders like to bring in people from their past or that are culturally similar to themselves. At the highest ranks, if a new leader comes in they will typically replace half their direct reports. Even if the CEO is promoted from within, the top performers at the next level will be forced to leave 1) because they were passed over and 2) in vying for the CEO position they likely burned bridges competing with the person who passed them over. This is why executives at that level have employment contracts stipulating that if they get fired, they are paid off handsomely.

The *Harvard Business Review*[7] reports that if the company's stock price goes up after the arrival of a new CEO, there is a 75 percent chance that one year later that CEO will still be in his or her job. But, if the stock price goes down, there is an 83 percent chance he or she will have been fired.

The demand to get immediate results is unrelenting. Few of us live under such daily, weekly, or monthly performance pressure. Rick Wallace says all this goes with the territory: "You're in a job that can go away or not, depending on how you perform. You'll keep it or you won't. If you don't perform well, you move on. It's not that complicated."

But even success is no guarantee. According to Chuck House and Ray Price in *The HP Phenomenon*, boards ask CEOs: "What have you done for me lately?" Shortly after generating record-breaking profits for their companies, boards fired John Akers, IBM; Ken Olsen, DEC; Ed McCracken, Silicon Graphics; and Rod Canion, Compaq.[8]

Those looking up to the CEO may see an imposing figure to be admired or feared. However, from the vantage point of the CEO, it's very different. Ginger Graham observed that CEOs often feel like "hired help." With shareholders demanding quarterly profits, and a board that understands little about the day-to-day problems of running the company, the CEO may feel like a puppet on a string with little job security.

Karen Sage suggests keeping your foot on the gas if you plan to move up:

At the executive level you are always upping the game higher and higher. If you don't, you're out. I hear people say, 'I got to the director level and I don't need to go any higher.' Usually those people are pushed out in a few years as aggressive up-and-comers show more promise. You always have to be upping your game and aspiring to the next level. You can stay at the same level if you are an individual contributor (though you still may be at risk of lower-cost workers replacing you), but in management you better be reaching for and achieving the next level or eventually people are going to push you out.

The Power Culture

According to researcher Adrian Savage, what gets you ahead at the lower levels is competence, but at the top it is all about raw power. In his breakthrough paper *"The Real Glass Ceiling,"*[9] Savage describes the shift that must happen as a manager advances up the ladder:

> As he or she crosses the invisible barrier, the rules change. To advance further, s/he must play by the new rules, even though they've probably never been explained or even acknowledged openly: succeed in getting and keeping a position of influence and power, from which to secure resources for his or her division or function. Do this amongst a highly competitive group of people who are all outstanding individuals, all working hard to secure their own positions and resources, and all committed to winning first and worrying about any casualties later, if at all.

Shortly after reading the Savage paper, an executive told me this story:

> I was giving my quarterly finance report to our top leadership. As had happened on three previous occasions, Mike, a peer from product development, began challenging my numbers in a derisive manner.
>
> I walked over to him, paused, and said: 'Mike, you do this to me every time I present. I am goddamned sick of it. This is my presentation and I plan to finish it. If you have something to say to me, you can do it after this meeting is over. But for now, I want you to shut up!'

This executive had played college football and presented an imposing figure. He said the room grew deathly quiet. Mike sank in his chair. "As I scanned the room, I could see looks of approval on the executives' faces," he told me. "Six months later, I was promoted to CFO. Two years after that, I was president of the company." Today he is CEO of a 10,000-employee Silicon Valley technology company.

In the C-suite, it is not about competence—that's a given. It is about power.

Self-Reliance

When you work with the top level, you're being watched for your leadership capabilities and potential. How savvy are you? How well do you pick up the cues? Can you be political without looking political? Keep in mind, there is no handbook or instruction manual for what to do. For example, the January, 2005 *Harvard Business Review* noted:

> Would-be CEOs can't expect much help in moving to the top spot. Boards and chief executives will give only the slightest indications of the behavior they expect. They want to see whether a candidate is sensitive to subtle cues and can adjust his or her behavior accordingly. CEOs and chairmen are more likely to test than to counsel.[10]

A recently promoted sales executive I worked with in a high-tech company felt he needed help in his new position. After a particularly contentious senior meeting, he approached the CEO complaining that he couldn't get things done without the CEO's support. The CEO said bluntly, "I don't have time for this. Okay, yes, you have my support. Now get on with it." The end.

Another example illustrates what Savage is describing. Dan was extremely talented and had moved quickly up the management ladder. He was on the verge of being promoted to the C-level. He complained to a VP I'd been working with that he'd presented an idea to the CEO and had been dismissed in an offhanded manner. The VP said, "Well, Dan, you know what, the CEO doesn't give a shit about your problems. He worries about things like shareholder value, what the financial analysts are going to say in their next quarterly report, some employee lawsuit, and a quality problem in the manufacturing facility in Taiwan."

The VP went on to add, "Now Dan, you may not like that, but it's not going to change. You may not be cut out to work at the C-level, and that's okay. There are lots of other places you can work. But if you are going to play at this level, that's the name of the game. So take care of yourself. The CEO isn't there to take care of you."

Looking for Empathy
in All the Wrong Places

A study by two University of California psychologists, Michael Krause and Dacher Keltner[11] indicates that people at the top of the economic food chain are less likely to be empathic. They are also less able to accurately read the emotions of others. On the other hand, lower-class people are more empathic and better able to read the emotions of others. According to Krause and Keltner, this is because lower-class people are more vulnerable in the unpredictable environments they live in. Hence, they need support from other people more than their upper-class counterparts.

When you're presenting in a Fortune 500 C-level meeting, you can bet your executive audience is in the upper class. In 2010 the mean compensation for S&P 500 CEOs was $12 million.[12] They are less likely to even notice the anxiety on your face, or to empathically acknowledge your job well done. So, be reassured, it is not personal.

From the *Harvard Business Review*, to high-tech companies, to the Adrian Savage research, a clear picture emerges: the higher up you go, the more self-reliant you must become. We might add to the old axiom: "It's lonely at the top—and, there's no help for you up there either." No wonder executive life coaching has become a $2.4 billion industry.

So what does all of this mean to you as you stand at the head of the big oval table about to deliver a career-defining presentation to a group of intimidating C-levels? The more you know about them, the more successful your presentation will be. First of all, remember that they are under enormous pressure to perform. They don't have time to chat, so get to the point. As Ginger Graham said, "I don't need your life story. I want to know why you're here, then let's get on with it." Secondly, if you do get treated in a rough manner, remind yourself that they are dealing with enterprise-wide problems, and the perceived rebuff is not personal.

It is hard not to take being grilled or even chastised by executives personally, especially if we bring childhood unresolved authority issues with us into the boardroom. Too often people enter the C-suite hoping for approval from a kind and loving "father figure." Such expectations muddy the water and make time-pressured executives annoyed.

The CEO Ain't Your Dad

> If you come in and seem angry or are being a "suck-up" looking for a reassuring pat on the head for doing a good job, then you are still working out your childhood authority issues. When we have to deal with all of that it is just a waste of our time.
>
> —Felicia Marcus

Our attitudes toward authority figures are determined by our childhood experiences with the first and most powerful authority figure in our lives, our fathers.

If you hated your mean authoritarian father, you may then unconsciously transfer that hatred to other authority figures in your life, like teachers, police officers, and bosses. On the other hand, if you had a distant and judgmental father whose acceptance you never got as a child, you may long for that approval from the boss, whomever that might be.

If all this sounds too "woo-woo" to you, hang on. It is very real in the boardroom according to the executives we interviewed. In fact, citing our research on this issue, *USA Today* ran a cover story about this problem on the front page of the Money section on Father's Day, June 6, 2007.[13]

Imagine a presenter at a C-level meeting with a serious authority problem like I just described. He or she, who may be 30 to 45 years old, walks into a room with a large mahogany table. Seated at the table is an imposing group of eight to 10 people in their 60s and 70s who perhaps founded the company, have enormous power, and huge net worths (perhaps in the hundreds of millions or

USA Today front page, Money section

even billions of dollars). If there was ever a time and place for childhood unresolved authority issues to surface, this is it.

This authority problem is so common that several executives expressed frustration over how it shows up in meetings. Whether the presenter is angry and rebellious or pleading for approval, these meetings are not the time or place for those issues to come up.

Ralph Patterson, former Product Line Manager at Hewlett-Packard in San Diego, told me about his aggravation when junior-level engineers came to his meetings looking for approval. Instead of presenting a recommendation based on their expertise, which is what he needed, they would spend a lot of time explaining how they did the experiment or the study and all the problems they had solved. His reaction was to hammer the presenters. "Don't tell me how you got the data," he'd say. "Tell me what the data means. We have to make a decision and move on."

To measure the extent of this problem, I asked our executives, "In your experience, what percentage of people presenting at the C-level have a collaborative attitude, have a needy attitude, or have an angry attitude?" They reported that a surprisingly high number of presenters, 34 percent, are looking for the reassuring pat on the head and are seen as "too needy." At the other end of the continuum, nine percent come across as angry and resentful. That leaves just 57 percent who have the collaborative attitude the executives value for getting the job done. The people in this last group don't feel either anger in the face of authority, or a pleading need for reassurance. Their locus of control is within themselves, not projected onto the

Cindy Skrivanek

external power structure around them. They collaborate with the executive team to solve business problems.

An excellent example of this comes from Cindy Skrivanek, at LSI Corporation, who speaks to her senior team all the time. She is clear about her role as a resource for decision making at the highest level:

I'm a tool of management. My job is to give senior executives information,

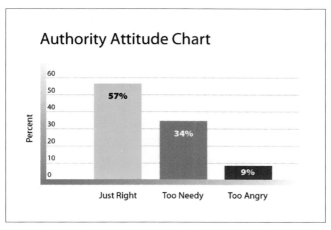

Figure 2.1 Authority Attitude Chart

lay out a set of options, or maybe ask for a decision . . . and then leave. I'm not there to be their buddy or to get pats on the back. A presentation isn't a personal development opportunity or a chance for increased visibility. I'm there to do a job. And that job is to help prepare the executives to make the best possible decisions for the company.

Putting all this together in what we might call an "Authority Attitude Chart," (Figure 2.1) you can see that only a little over half of the first-time presenters at the C-level handle authority issues with maturity. The executives were clear that these numbers apply to new presenters at the C-level. More seasoned presenters learn through experience how to be successful.

> The unforgivable sin is to come in and be arrogant and condescending to your boss. It is shocking how many people will come to me with work that's a piece of crap, and are arrogant about it . . . and if I don't like it that's my problem.
>
> —Felicia Marcus

Think about your own attitude when you present to the top level. If you are too needy for approval or too resentful of authority, work on moving toward a more collaborative approach. The executives will appreciate it, and you will be more successful.

You are asked to present at the meeting because you have something they need in the decision-making process. "I respect you or I wouldn't be asking you to be in the room," commented Brenda Rhodes. Do not be hurt if you don't get the approval you'd hoped for. Harold Fethe advised, "You may crave reassurance in the meeting, but you will almost certainly get higher marks if you can acknowledge their goodbyes, whether friendly or terse, and allow them to move on to their other work."

Executive Presence

> Business schools do not create leaders. You can only identify leaders. People are born that way.
>
> —Scott McNealy
> Co-Founder and Former CEO,
> Sun Microsystems

A relatively new concern in the leadership literature is "executive presence." Executives at the senior levels are all top performers, otherwise they would not be there. Some, though, get catapulted into the top spot. Executive presence plays a big role in such a promotion. Apparently top CEOs have it, and runners-up do not. What, exactly is "it?" What differentiates the stars from the superstars? Executive presence consists of a number of things, some physical, some social, some psychological. To meet Scott McNealy halfway, some of these skills are indeed inborn, but others can be learned.

In his book, *The Intangibles of Leadership*,[14] Richard Davis has an entire chapter on executive presence. Davis points out some of the physical aspects of executive presence: size, good looks, and athleticism. He also includes things that can be learned: speak slowly, walk tall, develop a firm handshake, and have strong eye contact. (The *Economist* magazine, reported that 30 percent of Fortune 500 CEOs are over 6'2" tall compared to just 3 percent of the U.S. population, and only 3 percent were under 5'7".)[15]

Although it's grossly unfair, Woody Allen is less likely to be the CEO than, say, Harrison Ford.

Other factors that contribute to executive presence are: confidence, charisma, ability to "own" the room, comfort with power dynamics, and social skills, i.e., the ability to make people feel at ease and feel heard. Think Bill Clinton. An Ivy League education also helps. Birth order may even play a role. A *USA Today*[16] survey, noted that 59 percent of CEOs are the first-born, confirming Scott McNealy's assertion.

Don Angspatt, a vice president at Symantec, added to this list by pointing out the impact of dress, "A well-tailored image is hugely helpful."

Figure 2.2 shows graphically the difference between the really effective C-level leader who does not become CEO, and the one who does.

Don Angspatt

Why should executive presence be important to you? For two reasons:

1. It is helpful to know the profile of what defines C-level executives so you know what is expected;
2. If you have ambition to get a seat at the table someday, these descriptors give you a menu of things to work on. (Sorry, can't be of much help on the height or birth order issues.)

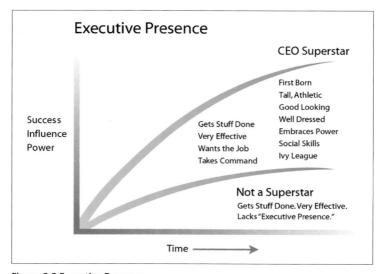

Figure 2.2 Executive Presence

C-Level Backgrounds

Looking over the class, family, and educational backgrounds of the executives in this study, we could see a pattern that fits a bimodal distribution curve. (Figure 2.3) Although this is not a scientific study, and the sample size is very small, what I noticed is that these executives fall into two quite different groups. One group grew up in very modest circumstances with parents who were not college educated. Others came from executive families with clear expectations about education and business success.

Ginger Graham observed:

> Most CEOs I've worked with came from modest means. It's about work ethic and sacrifice, and a desire to have influence and impact. You learn to work against adversity even though you don't have connections, means, or education. You have to get it done anyway.

Audrey MacLean recalled:

> Everything was a struggle. Nothing was handed to me. I didn't start with an inheritance, and an Ivy League pedigree, or a comfortable office. Everything I did was from scratch.

In one group, people knew early they would be in the world of business, and have executive roles. The other group found the executive calling later in life, usually because of mentors who were not their parents. It may be that people born into families in the middle are simply not that motivated, while

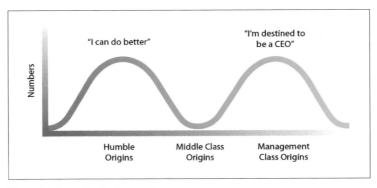

Figure 2.3 Executive Backgrounds

those at the top are groomed for it, and some at the bottom are strongly driven to make a better life for themselves.

Only in America

"Only in America are the streets paved with gold," said Steve Blank's mother. Steve elaborated, "My mother grew up in a hut. No electricity, no running water. She had to go to the well or the river. To go from that to Silicon Valley is one of those amazing journeys."

Steve's parents came to this country in steerage class, through Ellis Island to the lower east side of Manhattan and worked in the garment district. The son of immigrants, Steve started several companies, has become renowned for his entrepreneurial genius, and teaches in the business schools at Cal Berkeley and Stanford. All this in one generation.

California Congresswoman Anna Eshoo's parents came to the United States as youngsters. Her grandparents fled their native countries in the Middle East due to religious persecution. Anna became a member of the United States Congress in 1993. She said her parents really understood the blessings of this country:

> My father never once, in his entire life, complained about whatever he paid in taxes. Not once. If they had guests over to the house who started talking about politics and complaining about taxes, he'd say simply, 'They don't realize the blessings of this country.'

Dan Eilers' father was a truck driver with an eighth-grade education. Dan was CEO of three successful companies, and became a venture capitalist.

Ginger Graham grew up on a dirt farm in Arkansas. Her father was a rural mail carrier. She went on to get an MBA from Harvard, became CEO of several companies, taught at Harvard, and is a member of the Walgreens Board of Directors.

Felicia Marcus was raised by immigrant grandparents, got an undergraduate degree at Harvard, then earned a law degree. In her early 30s she was appointed by Los Angeles Mayor Tom Bradley to head the largest public works department in the country.

Brenda Rhodes grew up on a sugar beet farm in the state of Washington. She went on to found and become CEO of Hall Kinion, a very successful outplacement company. When she took her company public, Montgomery Securities said it was the most successful IPO of the year, raising $80 million.

These executives' stories rest four-square in the middle of what we call "The American Dream." They are bright, talented people who worked very hard to get where they are. Their stories attest to the remarkable opportunities this country offers. So as you address the people around that big oval table, keep in mind some of them may have remarkable backgrounds like these. They will likely appreciate the initiative you show.

Summary

- Are you a "tool of management," to use Cindy Skrivanek's concept? That is, are you clear that your role in top-level meetings is to help extremely talented, highly-stressed people make good decisions fast before moving on to the next decision?
- Do you realize that you may be treated dismissively and have your time cut in these meetings by people who are concerned with a lot more than you may even be aware of?
- Do you understand your presentation is not about getting a pat on the back or making friends with the executives sitting around the table? Or even, for that matter, getting a career boost?
- Are you capable of giving executives empathy about the lack of job security and unrelenting performance pressure that govern their lives?

If you can answer "Yes" to these questions, then you've captured the essence of this chapter. Gaining these insights about what life is like for people at the top gives you a huge advantage as you prepare and deliver senior-level presentations in the future. You are competing for limited resources with other mid-level people who also have good ideas. Your edge is that, as Sun Tzu says, you "know your enemy and yourself."

Part I Summary

In Part I, you met the executives of this story who serve as both the foils for our mid-level managers (whom you'll meet in Chapter 3) as well as their mentors. Your key takeaways in this book will be the strategies our managers learn as they struggle in their top-level presentations.

You also met Dick Anderson, the general manager of Hewlett-Packard's Computer Systems Division in Cupertino.

Remember, I didn't get what I wanted from him in that meeting. To confirm my memories of all this, I located Dick, who has retired to his ranch in Utah. He reviewed this manuscript and had some thoughts about our meeting back in 1983, as well as about the role of the CEO:

Dick Anderson

> The C-level can give you three things: time, money, and energy. What you really want from a CEO is his or her energy. It takes energy to accomplish anything. CEO energy takes many forms: creative thought energy, the energy to create a compelling vision, the energy to articulate a vision, the energy to convert nonbelievers, the energy to reward achievement, and the energy to lead.
>
> If no energy is expended, then nothing happens. It is easy to allocate a few bucks to some well-intended project, but if the project is not in line with where the boss is headed, it won't go anywhere. On the other hand, if an initiative is parallel to and supportive of the leadership's directions, the boss will add energy and use your initiative as one more engine to drive for success. Everybody wins.
>
> I saw quality as a compelling issue that needed more than my time, attention, or a few bucks for programs. It needed my energy. I also knew it would have to expand beyond my division and even beyond HP. In our meeting, *I must have concluded that you didn't show me how a few bucks in training could really move our quality results forward.*

There you have it. Dick Anderson had a big vision about quality, had been in the national media about the issue, and was looking for someone to help him move his agenda forward, but it sure as hell wasn't me. As a business neophyte, I was clueless about the bigger vision our GM had. My one exposure to our most senior executive went nowhere.

The rest of this book delves deeply into the issues facing senior-level people so that you will, unlike me, "have a clue" when you walk into that presentation room. You will hear from them what works and what does not work when you present at their meetings. You will learn critical skills about how to put a presentation together, as well as how to survive in a fast-paced senior meeting that you cannot control.

www.powerspeaking.com/chapter2

Survival Tactics
at the C-Level

I n Part I you met the people at the top. Part II takes you inside the boardroom where you get a ringside seat as six mid-level managers make presentations to top-level executives only to get shot down because they lack the key skills to be successful.

After getting advice from senior-level people they're given a second chance. Here is where the key learning happens. As you read about their successes, take note of the skills they learn from the executives. Those skills are the most practical and immediately useful takeaways from *Speaking Up®: Surviving Executive Presentations.*

CHAPTER

3

The Seven
Deadly Challenges

*For we have not even to risk the adventure
alone, for the heroes of all time have gone
before us . . .*

— Joseph Campbell
Mythologist

I n this chapter you will learn about seven presentation challenges that, if ignored, can run your presentation, and even
your career, right into the ditch. Not knowing what these challenges are and how to handle them is like going into the jungle
without a map, a compass, or a guide.

The situations we present here have brought even the best
mid-level managers to their knees. Why? Because they weren't
prepared. For example, one of our clients went on a disastrous
sales call with two unprepared colleagues:

> We went to IBM with our senior executive and a technical
> guy. We were visiting the number-one guy under the CEO.
> We were taken up to the penthouse meeting room. The IBM
> exec entered through a side door. He sat down and chatted
> with us for a few minutes. Then he looked at the three of us
> and said, 'So, what do you want from me?' We started trip-
> ping all over ourselves. Nobody had an answer. In fact, the
> technical guy started looking at his phone as if he had a call!
> The executive left. We lost the sale.

The Management Darwin Award

You may be familiar with the dark humor of the very popular Darwin Awards. They are posthumously given yearly to people who do such dumb things that they end up dead—thus removing themselves from the evolutionary food chain. In business, this notion might be modified slightly to be: The Management Darwin Award—an award you don't want to win. It would mean that you did something really dumb like walking into a C-level meeting unprepared, thus ending your successful career.

Evolution of the Seven Deadly Challenges

Over 300 eager mid-level managers crowded into a hotel ballroom to hear a panel of six C-level executives tell them bluntly—no holds barred—what they hate and what they love to hear from presenters. The date was November 18, 2002. It was our first "Speaking to the Big Dogs®" client event. Responding to input from the audience, the panel answered questions like:

- What do speakers do that irritates them?
- How and where do presenters fall short or lose their attention?
- What can presenters do to be successful presenting to decision makers?

Normally, we would be happy to see 30+ people attend one of our special events. With ten times that number, we knew this topic was addressing a huge unmet need.

During the seminar, we asked participants to list what throws them off track in their presentations to top-level executives. Seven categories emerged:

- Time Cut
- Disengaged Executives
- Food Fight
- Decision Maker Leaves
- Topic Change
- Side Talk
- Energetic Discussion

Rick, Steve Blank, Steve Kirsch, Corinne Nevinny.

Back row: Steve Kirsch, Corinne Nevinny, Bill Rossi, Jane Shaw. Front row: Steve Blank, Felicia Marcus.

The audience was transfixed as the executives explained what they could do to deal with these problems.

After that seminar, I conducted a series of videotaped interviews with C-levels to learn more about how presenters can avoid these problems. In January of 2004 we released an educational DVD of these interviews. Our DVD was recommended in the June, 2004 issue of *Fortune* magazine and won that year's "Best Award" from *Training + Development* magazine. The success of the DVD helped draw people to our training programs, and participants continue to share success stories about how the advice from the executives has helped them.

Training + Development magazine.

Soon, though, it became clear that something important was missing from the DVD: examples of actual C-level meetings. So we rented a television studio and re-created top-level meetings with 15 C-level executives and six mid-level managers discussing real business issues.

All six managers came prepared to deliver presentations they had given to their own company C-levels. During their presentations, they were confronted with one of the "Seven Deadly Challenges." They presented twice. They failed miserably the first time. Then they received corrective feedback

Television studios used to re-create top-level meetings.

Left to right: Dan Eilers, Steve Kirsch, Harold Fethe, Dan Warmenhoven, Corinne Nevinny, Robert Drolet.

Left to right, back row: John Kispert, Ned Barnholt, Felicia Marcus, Steve Blank, Greg Ballard. Front row: Mike Lyons, Vern Kelley, Brenda Rhodes. Missing: Audrey MacLean.

from the executives. Applying this new knowledge and skills, they were successful the second time around. This is where the learning happened.

The mid-level managers:

Andy Billings
Vice President,
Electronic Arts

Brent Bloom
Senior Director,
KLA-Tencor

Julie Patel
Senior Director,
Elan Pharmaceuticals

Sharon Black
District President,
Robert Half International

Randi Feigin
Vice President,
Juniper Networks

Todd Lutwak
Vice President,
eBay

In the following pages, we explore each challenge and each solution. You will learn the career-saving strategies recommended by the executives. Follow this advice and you will manage your next senior-level presentation like a pro.

Each of our six "heroes" has risen in the ranks of his or her organization and has achieved a high level of success. They are competent, adept professionals. Yet, they were still unprepared for the presentation challenges that lay ahead. In the following pages, you will take a seat at the table as they go on a career-wrecking or career-building adventure: presenting at a senior-level meeting.

Summary

Speaking Up®: Surviving Executive Presentations has evolved over time. Because of the generous contributions of executives and managers at all levels from a wide variety of companies, plus the insights and stories of participants in our various programs, it has become clear what the problems are, and what the solutions are.

In Chapters 4 through 11, we get very specific about what can go wrong and how to fix it. Pay close attention to the behavioral checklist at the end of each chapter. This is the information our six heroes learned the hard way. Apply these strategies and you can avoid the pain they went through.

Time Cut:
A $30,000/Hour Investment

If after 30 minutes they're on their third
slide, they have no concept of time, and no
respect for our time.

—Ned Barnholt

A lot is at stake when a presenter performs poorly in a top-level meeting. A valuable project may not get funding, a successful career can run off the tracks, and executives' time can be wasted.

The productivity cost of poor meeting performance can be measured in dollars and cents. Lots of dollars and cents. If we consider the top five leaders of a mid-sized company (CEO, CFO, COO, CTO, CMO, etc), with, let's say, $4 billion in revenue and calculate what it costs to put them into an hour-long meeting, the numbers are staggering. Their salaries, bonuses, stock options, and other perks can be determined from SEC public records. Our calculations indicate that having those five people in a decision meeting costs the shareholders more than $30,000 per hour! Assuming that this same group meets at least twice a week for hour-long meetings, the cost per year is $60,000/week x 52 weeks = $3.1M/year.

To make matters worse, CEOs report that the mean failure rate for the meetings they sit through is a whopping 67 percent. Almost 70 percent of these meetings are *total failures*! The cost of bad meetings to the shareholders is a cool $2.1 million, year in and year out ($3.1M x .67 failure rate). No wonder the pressure is so high to avoid wasting these executives' time.

According to Mike Lyons, corporate boards operate under a tenet called *duty of care*, that is, the board is charged with watching out for the shareholders' interests. You could assume that if a board knew the huge cost of poor presentations in front of the C-level, they would be expected to take action. Such losses could make the cost of your run-of-the-mill employee or shareholder lawsuit pale in comparison.

Mike Lyons

Flexibility

With so much at stake, you have to prepare for any and all contingencies. That means you have to be adaptable. You will crash and burn if you stick to your carefully rehearsed script and fail to appreciate the executives' concerns which span the entire business and can change moment to moment. They may be worried about what happened in finance, manufacturing, or quality assurance only minutes before you arrived.

Recall my presentation to Dick Anderson from Chapter 1. My meeting would have gone better that day had I been aware of his larger concerns. Demonstrating to C-level executives that you appreciate the scope of their responsibilities and that you can modify your presentation on the fly goes a long way toward helping you succeed.

As Harold Fethe, cautioned, "This group has to get tremendous decision volume through their meeting time together. They have horrendous travel schedules. The luxury of being together for meetings is

Harold Fethe

a daily, weekly, tense reality for these folks. You need to respect that and get up to that level of urgency."

As you walk into that room, be aware of the cost of the executives' time, the breadth of their concerns, and their expectations that a presenter will meet their shifting needs. Oracle VP Markus Zirn advises, "You have to literally throw out everything you learned from traditional presentation training. It's not about making a speech that educates, persuades, inspires, or leads. It's about raw decision making."

As we consider our first challenge, "Time Cut," you'll see that Todd Lutwak, Vice President, eBay, wasn't thinking about any of this. He was just focused on getting through the slide deck that had taken days to create. That mistake cost him dearly.

Todd Lutwak
Time Cut:
"I failed at the 99 yard line."

With an MBA from Northwestern University's Kellogg School of Management, Todd Lutwak's career in marketing has spanned 20 years.

When Todd walked into our senior-level meeting, he wanted approval for a new policy for the eBay seller community. He looked confident as he launched into the history of the program, but the executives immediately got restless. One executive didn't hide his frustration, "Todd, where are we going with this? What do we need to get done here? We've only got five minutes so let's get to the bottom line."

Oblivious, Todd responded, "I have seven slides we can get through. My team worked really hard on them and one of them has great visuals. You're going to love this slide." Exasperated, the executive got even more adamant, "Todd, what do you want from us here? Do you want us to give you a decision at the end of these seven slides?"

Todd continued to push his slide agenda. Bad move. "Why don't you give us the conclusions and we'll take a look at them?" a second executive said. "I don't understand the problem yet," complained a third executive.

Todd tried to punt by providing a little back story. The reprimand was sharp, "This is still strict chronology. Go to the problem and then peel it back if there's any time left." Unfortunately, Todd was already out of time. Having had enough, one executive announced that he had another meeting and abruptly left.

Todd envisions a legacy in which the people who worked for him over the years have fulfilling careers, and grow and evolve as people. As their boss, however, not delivering means that he's compromising their careers as well as his own.

Afterwards, Todd reflected on what went wrong, "When I got cut off, I felt it was a personal rejection. I wanted to go through my slides methodically: page one, page two, etc. They stopped me cold. The goal was to get the project approved. But I didn't get the message across in the time that was allotted, which has implications for me and my team down the road. It was as if my team got the ball down to the 99 yard line, and I failed to get it across the goal line."

Executive Advice

If you have half an hour on the agenda, plan on a 10 to 15 minute presentation. You're not going to get through it all because we're not going to let you. Remember, it's our meeting.

    —Dan Warmenhoven

Dispense with the slides and talk to us. Is there a decision you want from us?

    —Dan Eilers

You should know before you walk in the door—if I can only present three slides, which ones would they be?

    —Ginger Graham

By not anticipating questions and discussion, Todd showed he was simply not ready. When told he had a fraction of the time that he'd planned on, Todd should have adjusted his presentation immediately. He should have had one presentation for the length of time he had originally been given, and another five-minute presentation that spelled out the bottom line, why it was needed, the cost advantage, and the return on investment.

Todd's most important task was to be clear about what he wanted from the group and then respond to their concerns. When they got antsy about the timing, he should have let go of his script, and gone directly to his elevator pitch (see following page). That would have addressed the executives' concerns about timing.

Elevator Pitch

A board member will often ask, "What's the elevator pitch?" If you can't reduce your strategy or proposition down to a few sentences that can be described in an elevator going just ten floors, then you probably don't have a central message that is succinct and compelling.

    —Greg Ballard

Time Cut
Framework for the Elevator Pitch (PREP)

Goals for the Elevator Pitch:

- Net out key elements of your message
- Provide a high-level summary
- Define a clear, compelling reason to hear more
- Focus on benefit / value

P Position (Bottom Line)

R Reason (Key Point)

E Evidence (Data)

P Position (Bottom Line)

Figure 4.1 PREP Model.

Be prepared with an elevator pitch for every presentation you make. Use the PREP structure:

- **(P) Position (bottom line)**
  One sentence statement explaining what you want and the Return On Investment (ROI).
- **(R) Reason**
  Short explanation of why your bottom line is important to the company.
- **(E) Evidence**
  Example or one piece of evidence supporting your case.
- **(P) Position (bottom line)**
  Repetition of what you want.

The elevator pitch is deemed so important in today's business world that MIT has a yearly contest for its engineering students based on the elevator pitch. Winners walk away with a $20,000 cash prize.

No Pages at All

After getting executive advice, Todd realized he needed to be more flexible and able to make changes on the spot in response to their time constraints. Next time through, that's just what he did. At the executives' request, he got to the point, wrapped up, asked for the order and got it. The meeting then proceeded to the next item on the agenda.

He reflected, "The second time I went in, I was prepared for a 1-minute presentation, a 10-minute presentation, and 4-minute presentation, whatever. I could have gone to page one, page seven, page two, or no pages at all. I was ready for whatever happened."

Being prepared with options is critical. Because Todd was ready with his elevator pitch, and could cut as necessary, he got what he wanted despite having his presentation time slashed once again.

Summary

To avoid the traps of the Time Cut:
- Expect to get your time cut
- Know your goals for the meeting and your bottom line
- Come prepared with a much shorter version of your presentation
- Be prepared with an elevator pitch
- Choose three slides that will deliver your message
- Be ready to let go of your rehearsed script and go immediately to your bottom line

www.powerspeaking.com/chapter4

CHAPTER

5

Disengaged Executives:
It's You or The Smartphones

*Type A personalities have short attention
spans. They get bored. So you've got to
keep moving. Pace is as critical as content.*
—Dan Warmenhoven

J ulie Patel, Senior Director, Elan Pharmaceuticals, was just
three minutes into her presentation when she noticed out of
the corner of her eye that several executives were fiddling
with their smartphones. She ignored it. She certainly had plenty else to worry about in this critical presentation. She thought
to herself, "Surely this will pass. They must see how important
it is that we move ahead on this proposal."

Things got worse. No one seemed to be paying attention
as Julie continued, "Our leaders need this program in these
tough economic times. We're
not able to compensate people
appropriately." The executives
ignored her as they continued
to text and talk on their phones.

Frustrated, Julie suddenly
imagined pulling a hammer
out of her briefcase and smashing all the executives' smartphones as she shouted, "Maybe
now you'll pay attention!"

Pure fantasy. It was all a dream.

The second deadly challenge requires making sure from the beginning that the executives are engaged, then keeping them engaged, and drawing them back in if they become distracted. Finally, if none of that works, you need to get your sponsor involved. *(We'll talk more about the crucial role of your sponsor in Chapter 11.)*

Julie Patel
Disengaged Executives
"It's been a rough day."

With a 21-year career in HR functions with companies involved in the life sciences, Julie Patel has worked on several organization change integrations developing talent through mergers and acquisitions. She works to ensure that human resource strategies are consistent with business objectives. She cares deeply about the human side of the business.

Julie went into the senior-level meeting hoping to get a commitment for investment in the company's key talent at a cost of $200,000. As the senior team got more and more distracted with emails and their cell phones, she felt increasingly disheartened. "I really need your support and attention on this," she pleaded. The executives remained engaged with everything except her proposal.

Julie's first mistake was that she failed to get and hold their attention. She needed to start by confirming the value of the topic as well as the time allotted, and then get to the point

quickly to keep executives engaged. When they became distracted, she should have done a process check, i.e., reconfirmed the agenda.

Julie's next mistake was assuming that the executives had tuned her out just because they were looking at their cell phones instead of at her. Many executives have turned multitasking into an art form. They can check their smartphone, look at their computer, and hear what you're saying all at the same time.

Finally, Julie could have used her sponsor's help to re-engage everyone because the sponsor can address the group in a way she cannot.

When it was over, back in her office, Julie stared off into the distance. "It was a disaster. Because of my lack of impact with them, they're going to miss the opportunity to do something powerful for the employees. For all the preparation, and the time of everyone in the room, and to not get the outcome I wanted . . . Well, it's been a rough day."

Executive Advice

Get engagement. That's what you're looking for. If you don't have it at the beginning, stop and get it. If you never get it, go home.

—Brenda Rhodes

If your audience seems to be disengaged, one of two things may be happening: 1) They are, in fact, distracted and not paying attention to your presentation; or 2) They are using their computers or other devices to do something that relates to the information you're presenting, i.e., jotting down an important point you made or calling a colleague to invite them to the meeting. So, don't jump to conclusions. They may in fact be in support of your proposal.

—Felicia Marcus

If you can connect your problem with what we're trying to do, that gets our attention much faster.

—Mike Lyons

Still Relevant?

Julie's second presentation went much better. Upon noticing that the executives all seemed checked out, instead of giving up, she asked for a verbal confirmation (a process check) to confirm that the agenda was still important. "Is this still a relevant topic? Should I continue or does something else need to happen here?" Her question forced the executives to make a conscious decision about where the meeting was going. The one-two punch helped recapture their attention.

She also enlisted her sponsor's help, a plan they had already agreed upon should things get rough. That helped re-engage the executives and made for a much more successful outcome.

After it was over, Julie said, "It went much better this time. I read the room, did a process check, and brought in my sponsor for help. Bottom line, the group was bought in. They were engaged. They were interested. They were asking questions, and I got what I wanted!"

Summary

To avoid the traps of Disengaged Executives:

- Make sure you confirm the topic and time up front, and get right to your bottom line request

If you notice the executives are losing focus:

- Don't make assumptions about what's happening
- Read the room and take action
- Re-engage with a question
- Do a process check confirming the value of the topic
- Enlist your sponsor's help

www.powerspeaking.com/chapter5

CHAPTER

Food Fights:
You Are Not the Referee

The war between R&D and Sales &
Marketing was vivid and alive in every
discussion and every moment. The pot
shots, the digs, the opportunities to take
advantage or to prove a point among the
top executives—all this is very real.

—Ginger Graham

B ack in my high-tech corporate days representing Quality Assurance, I sat in meetings that included people from R&D and Sales & Marketing. The groups didn't like each other. Someone would make a snide comment, then another. In several meetings, it escalated to shoving and chair throwing. Clearly something much deeper was going on here besides surface discussion about, say, delaying the release date of a new software upgrade. All this anger and resentment had the feeling of a schoolyard brawl. I knew people like this in junior high and high school.

For example, in high school there was a group of kids— mostly boys—who were in the math club. They were armed with slide rules on their belts (back in my day), wore glasses and didn't have dates on Saturday night. Guess what happened to them? They got PhDs and ended up in corporate R&D departments.

Then there was another group of boys. Good looking, socially at ease, jocks, and class officers. They were cool. They got all the good looking girls. Guess what happened to them? They earned MBAs and ended up in corporate sales and marketing departments.

Now these two groups found themselves sitting across the table trying to work together on some new product release. They didn't like each other in junior high and high school, and they still don't. I heard comments like: "Those people in marketing don't have a clue how this stuff works. They just play golf and go to lunch with clients." Or, conversely, "Nothing happens until somebody sells something. These R&D geeks couldn't talk to a customer if you put a gun to their head." And so it went.

It is just this kind of deep-seated suspicion of people from other functional groups that can cause a food fight to erupt for no apparent reason. You get 10 people around a table who are all strong-willed, extremely bright, and have a huge depth of knowledge in their particular area, and they start jockeying for position: money, power, turf, resources. Pretty soon a full blown food fight erupts over something that has nothing to do with what you're presenting.

Here, the role of the CEO is like the teacher in the schoolyard—get these kids to play cooperatively together. As Ginger Graham noted, "These are two different operating styles. We need both the analytic and passionate views, and a good management team will have both." Getting them to work together is the real trick.

Without direct power or authority over these people, your role is to listen, attempt to refocus the group, and failing that, enlist your sponsor's help. In our next challenge, the Food Fight, Brent Bloom, Senior Director, KLA-Tencor, had to deal with people yelling at each other about issues completely unrelated to his presentation. Arguments erupted about the money being spent on training and the assertion that training can never be a profit center. It went on and on. Brent simply was not prepared for it.

Brent Bloom
Food Fight:
"It was like a death spiral."

Brent Bloom started his career at KLA-Tencor in 1986. He initially worked in engineering-related jobs focusing on hardware and software support. He was soon promoted to management roles that gave him exposure to the senior executives. He moved on to leadership positions in training and development. Brent frequently presents to KLA-Tencor's top-level executives.

Brent's objective was to get funding for a "media management tool." He anticipated that the meeting would include all the top leadership of the company, and the topic could prove contentious. Additionally, he knew that with limited funds there would be tough questions asked about how this project fit into the bigger picture.

"As with any organization, the leaders are fighting for resources for all kinds of projects, so there may be some discussion around where this project falls in importance compared to some of the other projects that are up for funding," Brent said before the presentation. "You always hope that things go calmly but you never know. This is definitely something that will create some dialogue and passionate debate, so I need to be prepared for that."

Brent had barely established the timeframe for the presentation and its subject matter when the heated discussion he had anticipated erupted into a rip-roaring executive food fight. As the executives verbally assaulted each other in an apparent turf war, Brent made a couple of feeble attempts to refocus the group, but to no avail. He could barely get a word in edgewise.

As the verbal battle escalated, Corinne Nevinny, loudly asserted, "This is about revenue enhancement, not cost containment!" Then Robert Drolet shot back at her, "This is just another of Dan's pet projects," and it went downhill from there.

"What the hell do I do now?" Brent wondered. Despite being well prepared even to the point of anticipating a volatile reaction, he had lost control. Finally he just gave up. Shoving his hands in his pockets, he looked from one side of the conference table to the other like a spectator watching a tennis match.

"That didn't go like I'd planned," he said afterwards. "I had a short presentation that laid out the key points and next thing I know, it's out of control, and they're going all over the place with the conversation. It seemed like I was in a hole and they kept shoveling dirt in on top of me. It felt like a death spiral."

Brent's sponsor did not come to his aid, and Brent's lack of engagement with the executives hurt him. "A lot of presentation success comes down to the way you keep the flow, the style, and the interpersonal dynamics of the presentation on the right track," said Bryan Lamkin. Brent failed on that front.

Executive Advice

You don't want to get into a fight between the C-levels. You're not going to win that.

—Mike Lyons

If the sponsor doesn't step in and save it, then the presenter is at a loss.

—Robert Drolet

What you don't want to do is for both you and your sponsor to sit back and let it happen.

—Steve Kirsch

The food fight is definitely a tricky business. Timing is important. The presenter must try to regain focus, but not interrupt too soon. When Brent saw the discussion was getting overheated, very lengthy, and off track, he needed to assert himself and take action, but instead he backed away from the table and looked timid. It was up to him and/or his sponsor to grab hold of a specific concern voiced in the group and address it before the executives started going at each other. That way, at least the fight would have been focused around Brent's agenda.

As Mike Lyons commented, "If heat is coming because C-level executives don't agree with each other, then all you can do is try to accurately reflect the positions you hear being expressed, make a recommendation, then stand back and let them decide."

Contributing to the Process

After getting advice from the executives about how to manage a food fight, Brent did a dry run of his presentation in front of his sponsor. His sponsor peppered him with some of the challenging questions he could expect. Brent also made sure he was clear on the various viewpoints held by individual executives and how they might react to his proposal. He got assurance that he could count on his sponsor's support in the meeting. As Brent observed, "My sponsor has a lot more credibility with this group than I do."

These preparations were critical. During his do-over, Brent was ready for whatever direction the questions might take depending on what the executives started to talk about. So he was able to focus on the concerns voiced by the various executives before honing in on one that seemed most pertinent. By addressing a particular concern in detail, he stopped the food fight before it got going and demonstrated that he knew what

he was talking about. That proved the difference between success and failure.

After his second presentation Brent commented, "It felt good to have a deep discussion with the executive team. It made me feel like I was making a contribution to their decision process." (Recall Cindy Skrivanek's "I'm a tool of management" quote, Chapter 2, p. 22.)

The executives were most impressed with his bearing. He could connect with them because he had "executive presence" (see Chapter 2). He was well-dressed, held his ground, and was forceful without being too aggressive in handling questions. Robert Drolet liked how he "stepped up to the table and plugged into the conversation." Dan Eilers commented, "Your demeanor was perfect. You stood your ground and you did it with a pleasant, likable temperament." In a word, Brent's executive presence made all the difference.

Summary

To avoid the traps of a Food Fight:

- Present with executive presence
- Listen for the issues
- Move toward the group
- Handle objections
- Do a process check
- If all else fails, engage your sponsor

www.powerspeaking.com/chapter6

CHAPTER

7

Decision Maker Leaves:
Reading the Room

You need to be cognizant of people's eye-balls, all of them around the room.

—Steve Blank

I f you're starting to feel like you need to be a juggler to successfully present at the C-level, you're not far off. And one of those balls you can't lose track of, according to Steve Blank, is the ability to "understand when the context of the meeting has shifted around you and be able to move from 'presentation mode' into 'process mode'." Instead of focusing on content, you may need to take off your "presenter hat" and put on your "process hat." That is, you stop to make sure that the way you are presenting your content is hitting the target. Presenters who can make this distinction will have a huge advantage at senior-level meetings.

Unfortunately, many presenters are so focused on their content that they don't have the psychological bandwidth to be aware of what is going on in the room on an interpersonal level:

- Who is paying attention?
- Who is not?
- Who is taking it into the weeds?
- Who has time constraints?
- Who is being argumentative?
- Who is being supportive?

The list goes on and on. An effective top-level presenter has a kind of meeting ESP that allows him or her to constantly scan the room and make adjustments as necessary in real time.

He or she is able to read the room and modify the flow of the content as necessary to accommodate changes in the moment. That skill is at the heart of facilitation.

Fail to notice what is going on in the room, like when the boss leaves in the middle of your presentation, and your presentation will be in big trouble. It happened to Sharon Black, District President, Robert Half International.

Sharon Black
Decision Maker Leaves:
"I'm very disappointed in myself."

As a senior district president for RHI, Sharon oversees operations throughout northern and central California, Hawaii, Nevada, and Utah. She has been in the staffing industry for more than 25 years, and has held high-level positions in several other Bay Area staffing firms. She has been in her current position for four years.

In her presentation, Sharon's goal was to get approval to hire a team of people to help the company work with their new subsidiary. If the executives approved this program, the revenue increase for the company would be about $25M, a huge ROI. Sharon expected most of the C-levels would be there, but especially the CEO who was critical to the decision-making process.

During the meeting, which was attended by Sharon's boss as well as her mentor, Sharon sat at the head of the table in front of her computer immersed in the data. She hadn't even gotten

through her third point when the CEO gestured to one of the executives across from her, whispered something to him, and then left the room. Sharon failed to notice.

The CEO's departure had to be brought to her attention. "What would you like me to do?" Sharon asked, her composure clearly rattled. The rambling, unfocused discussion among the remaining executives at the table after the CEO left made things worse. Sharon did not get the clear decision she wanted. She knew she'd blown it "I was so focused on my content that I was not aware of what else was happening around the room. I was not watching what the audience was doing. I did not notice when the CEO left the room, and she's the decision maker. Honestly, I'm very disappointed in myself."

Sharon's first faux pas was sitting down with the executives. Taking a seat at the head of the table made things much worse. That's the power position. Instead of being appropriately deferential, Sharon had inadvertently signaled disrespect by assuming the role of an equal rather than that of a presenter. Of course, sitting rather than standing wasn't her only mistake.

Executive Advice:

If I get up to leave, I prefer that they stop me and ask, 'Do you want to continue?' or 'What do we need to do here?'
—Brenda Rhodes

Don't assume you can't get a decision. Most of the time the key decision maker is unwilling to hold up a consensus just because he or she had to duck out for something.
—Harold Fethe

During the meeting, Sharon needed to be aware that she was about to lose her audience and address that instead of focusing so intently on her slides. At the beginning of the meeting, she should have acknowledged the CEO's attendance. Simply saying, "Brenda, thank you for joining us," would have made it more difficult for Brenda to slip away.

Paying Attention
Pays Off

When Sharon did her presentation a second time, she stood up. This allowed her to read the room and tune into to her audience's nonverbal communication. She said, "I made sure that they were engaged with me, not looking at their smartphones." When Brenda got up to leave, Sharon noticed what was happening.

"Brenda, I see you have to leave. What would you like me to do?" she asked, interrupting her own presentation. "I'd be happy to reschedule for another meeting, or wait until you come back." Brenda simply asked that she pause for a moment until she returned. This time around, the meeting ended successfully for Sharon.

Summary

To avoid the traps of Decision Maker Leaves:
- Read the room
- Focus on the decision maker
- Ask the decision maker what to do as he or she is getting up to leave
- Check with the group about what to do if the decision maker hasn't made it clear

www.powerspeaking.com/chapter7

CHAPTER

8

Topic Change:
Time to Improvise

*I don't know why we're spending time on
this when the fundamental problem is the
product structure.*

—Dan Warmenhoven

P resentations at the top level can change directions mid-stream. That's not surprising considering who's involved, what's at stake, and the fact that they're often more like guided discussions than structured lectures. What should you do when the executives want to address a different topic? You'll find your answer in jazz. Yes, jazz. Like a jazz musician, your ability to improvise in the heat of the moment may be the difference between success and failure.

Eddie Harris

Jazz saxophone player, Eddie Harris (1934–1996), told me in a 1976 interview, "Jazz is a business. I have to read the audience. If I'm playing far out, and I see they want a ballad, I'll change in the middle of the tune." Business presenters should take their cue from Eddie Harris. Should topics switch in the middle of your presentation, be prepared to go with the flow.

When we think of improvisation, we think of jazz and comedy clubs. Improv comedy involves themes provided on the spur of the moment from the audience. Similarly, jazz improvisation occurs in the moment as the players "riff" off of each other. We don't think of high-level business meetings being improvisational, or off the cuff. But, in fact, the most creative business solutions

61

often evolve from improvisational interactions. Jazz metaphors are not uncommon in business:

Mike Lyons

From a CEO: Mike Lyons uses a jazz metaphor to explain business interactions, "As a CEO, I have to let everyone play. You can't run them over. See what melody they come up with and play with that. Otherwise, why are they there? Don't shut them down. It becomes a bad place to work."

Akira Tana

From a Jazz Drummer: Akira Tana recalled, "Miles Davis was a great CEO of a jazz company. He allowed people to express themselves and to contribute, and it nurtured them. Many went on to become leaders of their own groups."

From a Corporate VP: Mark Shaw, former VP of HR with Applied Materials, facilitated high-level decision meetings. "In board meetings I think of the CEO's staff as band members," he told me. "So, what is the dynamic of the CFO and CEO? They are key players. What are they saying to me? I'm trying to incorporate their pieces into the 'music' that is being played in the room. For example, we were having a financial crisis. I was trying to hear what the CFO was saying and link it to what the CEO was saying. I was trying to get all the players on the same page about what had to happen. We were all in the same band."

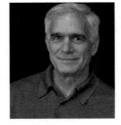

Mark Shaw

From a State University: The business school at San Francisco State University brings jazz improvisation into the business community to help business leaders loosen up the decision processes. The program is called, "Jazz at Work." Here is how they describe the improvisational parallels between jazz and business:

Jazz is an exciting metaphor for high performance organizations. It's a collective and improvisational art form based on high levels of team creativity. Businesses today are without a score to play by, and managers need to learn to think like the best jazz musicians. Lessons from jazz can teach businesses how to improvise, manage change, and drive innovation in real time.

> *From the Harvard Business Review:* 'The best team leaders are like jazz players, improvising as they go along.'[1]

If improvisation is so powerful, why don't we hear more about it in business? The answer: fear. Like the presenter who cannot let go of the PowerPoint slides, many in business fear that a free-form meeting will spiral out of control. However, all indications are that in most corporate environments it is far riskier to do nothing. Robert Lutz, former Vice Chairman of General Motors, and a noted creative force in the car industry advised, "The biggest risk is no risk at all."

For Randi Feigin, Vice President, Juniper Networks, the biggest risk proved to be her inability to follow the lead that the executives set.

Randi Feigin
Topic Change
*"I felt so alone and out there,
so vulnerable. It was horrible."*

In her 12 years with Juniper, Randi has held two other VP positions: Business Process Reengineering and Investor Relations. Randi's goal in the meeting was to get executive buy-in, endorsement, and support for a new company-wide program. She worried about the executives' demands to "keep it at a high level," and at the same time to go deep and clarify all the details.

Unfortunately for Randi, her topic wound up triggering other executive concerns. As she was enumerating why people would potentially resist the change she was proposing, they stopped listening and spun off in other directions. Instead of leading the presentation, Randi found herself sidelined and barely able to get a word in edgewise.

"Can we maybe go back to the slides?" she finally asked tentatively during a lull in the discussion swirling around her. Her request was shot down just as completely as her efforts to get their approval for the program she was pitching.

Reflecting on her initial failure, Randi said, "No matter what I did, I couldn't get them back on track to focus on my proposal." Because she didn't get the support she needed, she felt the program was going to fail. By the end, she was totally demoralized.

The problem she was trying to solve wasn't the problem that the executives were interested in solving. But Randi simply couldn't switch directions. To make things worse, her sponsor let her flounder instead of jumping in.

Executive Advice:

All 'big dogs' aren't equal. You have to pick up on where the biggest dog is headed. You have to be willing to abandon your presentation, pick up on that conversation, and try to lead it to where you want to go.

—Robert Drolet

If the presenter is a more junior person, the only person who can get it back on track is the sponsor.

—Dan Eilers

Let people have the back-and-forth dialogue, but then be attentive to when it is the right time to jump back in to get people back on topic. The best way to do that is to look to your sponsor for help.

—Corinne Nevinny

When the executives veered from the topic Randi wanted to discuss, it was because they felt something more pressing had to be resolved before they could consider her proposal. The challenge for Randi was to recognize the issues the executives thought were important and to address them head on. She and her sponsor needed to find the right moment to jump into the discussion, deal with the questions, and then clarify the next step, i.e., redirect the discussion, postpone it, or make a follow-up plan.

Sponsor's Help

After getting executive advice, Randi's second presentation was a success. When the executives went off topic and brought up detailed product issues, she took a more assertive approach and stepped in with a direct response. When that failed, she appealed to her sponsor for help. He was able to redirect the conversation and she got what she wanted.

Randi commented, "I wanted to step in, but was concerned about being too aggressive. So I looked to my executive sponsor for support because he's allowed to be more aggressive." That helped refocus the group and win the day.

Summary

To avoid the traps of Topic Change:
- Acknowledge the topic change
- Handle objections
- Get help from your sponsor
- Agree to follow up

www.powerspeaking.com/chapter8

Side Talk:

Keeping Your Poise

*Rickey and Suki, do the two of you have
something you'd like to share with the rest
of the group?*

—Rick's third grade teacher, her voice dripping with
sarcasm in order to embarrass the two side talkers

D oesn't it really bother you when a couple of executives begin having a sidebar conversation during your presentation? It's something that's not only distracting for you as the presenter, but it also distracts the rest of the people around the table. There are some ways to deal with this. Unless you're actively trying to limit your career, however, direct confrontation is not one of them.

Andy Billings, VP, Electronic Arts
Side Talk:
*"I lost my patience with them.
We didn't get the green light."*

Andy Billings is Vice President of Profitable Creativity (Organizational Effectiveness and Leadership Development), and has been with Electronic Arts for 14 years. He has a PhD in behavioral psychology with an emphasis in organizational change.

Andy's presentation to the executives was a proposal to change the ways new products are developed to increase both creativity and profitability. He knew that it would be great for revenues, great for margins, and great for the company's engineering talent. In short, it was a win-win-win.

He had barely begun when two executives started having a sidebar conversation. He tried to ignore it, but instead, he lost

his cool. "Hey guys, what is sooo important that the two of you can't pay attention to this presentation and make a decision?" he challenged aggressively.

He certainly got them to stop talking, but the sarcastic smack-down was definitely not well-received. "I think we've heard more than enough," one of the executives said with disdain after a few more exchanges.

Andy reflected later, "Boy did that confrontation feel good in the moment . . . Unfortunately I didn't get what I wanted. What a mistake."

Reflecting on his belligerent misstep Andy explained that 15 other people across the company were depending on him to deliver. "So now we have all the business units and the cross-functional teams stalled. It will be hard to get this project teed up again. This didn't help my career at all." Not only did Andy not manage to score or even move the ball forward, he earned himself a monster penalty.

Executive Advice

When speaking to the top level, you can't shush your audience.

—Audrey MacLean

It connotes arrogance if the presenter says, 'Can I please have your attention,' so it's better if the sponsor pulls them back in.

—Corinne Nevinny

If the sponsor or the CEO notices we're not getting people's attention on this important decision, then it's best for the sponsor to call time out to refocus the group.

—Ned Barnholt

It's never appropriate to lose your temper with executives. When two people in the meeting began to have a sidebar conversation, Andy had several options. He could have ignored them and focused his attention on the person responsible for making a decision on his project. Or he could have stopped for a moment of silence in an attempt to regain their attention. He could also have done a group check-in, i.e., "Does this make sense to you? Am I on the right track?" He could have called on one of the people talking and asked for an opinion on his presentation. Failing all this, Andy could have asked his sponsor for help.

A Better Approach

For his second presentation, Andy used a gentler approach to re-engage the side talkers by politely calling one by name and asking for an opinion on his proposal. When that didn't work, he turned to his sponsor for help, "Ned, maybe you can help me—do you think we're on track in the discussion?" That allowed his sponsor to bring the attention back to his presenta-

tion. Andy was heard, and he was able to go back to his team with the news that they could now move forward. "I think what I did better the second time around was just let the executives have their meeting. When they were ready, they came back to what I wanted to do. I didn't lose my poise and I got what I wanted."

Summary

To avoid the traps of Side Talk:
- Do not use direct confrontation
- Politely re-engage
- Appeal to your sponsor

www.powerspeaking.com/chapter9

10

The Energetic Discussion:
Less Talking and More Listening

A person who is truly understanding, who takes the trouble to listen to us as we consider our problem, can change our whole outlook on the world.

—George Elton Mayo
Harvard Business School, 1926–1947

S ometimes your presentation can go so well that the executives are completely engaged. They are totally with you. Ideas are flying around. They are building on each other's suggestions. We call this the "Energetic Discussion." Your challenge is to listen well and not to miss anything.

Since most books on management and leadership stress the importance of listening, mid-level managers who attend our training sessions often believe they do it well. Not true. They are amazed at how poorly they listen when we get into exercises that teach this vital skill. Listening is not easy, yet it is central to facilitating a high-level conversation. Conversely, not listening because you're so focused on your presentation can derail a successful career.

As a CEO, John Kispert noted:

> I listen, 24/7. That's my job. Nothing is more insulting or annoying to an executive than to ask a question and have the person provide the answer that's

in their head without even addressing what's being asked because they never really heard the question.

Why Is Listening So Hard?

If listening is so important, why don't business people do it better? First of all, we aren't taught how. We are taught to argue and debate. This is especially true in engineering and science university education. You have to defend your work, and conversely, poke holes in your opponent's design.

Secondly, we are often not listening because we're thinking ahead to what we're going to say next. According to Greg Ballard, "The most common flaw I see in junior people is when they're quiet, they're not really listening to what I'm saying; they're thinking about what they're going to say next. That's a big mistake." This keeps us from hearing what the person is really saying.

Finally, as psychologist Carl Rogers (1902–1987) has pointed out, if we really listen to the other person at a deep empathic level, we run the risk of being changed in the process. He developed an entire school of psychotherapy built around "active listening" called "Client-Centered Therapy." Rogers and his followers went on to apply these ideas to business, parenting, and even international relations. For his work with opposing sides in South Africa and Northern Ireland, Rogers was nominated for a Nobel Peace Prize in 1987. Rogers observed:

> Very rarely do we permit ourselves to understand precisely what the meaning of the other person's statement is to him or her. I believe this is because understanding is risky. If I let myself really understand another person, I might be changed by that understanding. And we all fear change. So it is not an easy thing to permit ourselves to understand an individual, to enter thoroughly and completely and empathically into his or her frame of reference.[1]

Building Trust

Empathic listening is a rare thing, especially in business. When we *do* hear about listening in business, it's usually connected with management and leadership skills. The question then becomes: "Why would a speaker need listening skills? They're supposed to do the talking." The answer: to build trust.

Remember, in the C-suite, ideally two-thirds of the time is spent in discussion. Opinions and questions are flying around. There are hidden agendas, horse trading, and arm wrestling over financial issues. If you want this group to approve your request, building their trust is the super highway to getting what you want. In an ambiguous, conflict-laden disagreement among the top leaders, the person who can show understanding and even empathy for the divergent positions—the person who has really listened—will be seen as more trustworthy. Letting people know you've heard their divergent positions will help to build that trust.

> The higher up you go, the more comfortable you must be with ambiguity.
>
> —Mark Milani,
> VP, Oracle

In the give and take of a high-level meeting, listening is critical. Only by really listening can you have a dialogue, and the dialogue increases your believability. Getting the executives engaged in an energetic discussion may be the most important overall key to your success. To do that successfully, you must be able to facilitate the discussion, and that means listening well and being able to read the room. That is just what Andy Billings did in his second presentation.

Andy Billings
Energetic Discussion:
We had a spirited debate and I came away with a couple of new ideas that I otherwise would not have had.

We also had Andy present his new product development proposal while dealing with the Energetic Discussion challenge. In this situation, the executives are totally engaged and the only "distraction" is that the ideas are flying around at lightning speed. The presenter is challenged not to miss anything.

Knowing when and how to step into a lively discussion and steer it your way demands agility, flexibility, and sensitivity. Capture the ideas, confirm your understanding by repeating what you hear, and be light on your feet so you can follow the discussion. Good listening skills and improvisation are key.

Executive Advice

If I feel like you're lecturing me, then I tune out and don't have much confidence in you. But if you're listening, engaging, dialoguing, and we're having a good discussion, then I have a lot more confidence that you understand your subject.

—Ned Barnholt

It's important to let people have their conversations with each other because they are the dynamic team that is leading the organization.

—Felicia Marcus

Moving Forward

By using high-level listening skills, Andy facilitated a rich discussion among the executives. Not surprisingly, he felt good about the presentation:

The discussion went very well. Not only did we get the okay to move forward, we got them really engaged in the conversation. When they're talking and debating and having conversations between pairs and trios, that's their way of thinking it through. When the executives are talking, they're getting used to the idea, and you're selling. When you have to do a lot of talking, you're not selling.

Steve Blank commented, "Andy kept summarizing, 'Here's what I heard you say.' That is an incredibly effective technique to pull all the strands together and move the meeting forward." Andy explained his reasoning, "When you summarize what people have said, it acknowledges their concerns, and they can feel comfortable that the issues they raised will be addressed." Andy was able to move the group forward by facilitating the discussion. He ably applied the listening and improvisation skills that we'll explore further in Part III.

Summary

To be successful facilitating an Energetic Discussion:

- Listen well
- Capture the issues
- Accept executive input
- Outline the next steps

www.powerspeaking.com/chapter10

Part II Summary

Until now, there's been no rule book for how to succeed in top-level presentations. Now you have one. C-level executives are demanding high-achievers, who are constantly in a time crunch. In Part II they gave our mid-level presenters advice about how to handle the "Seven Deadly Challenges,"

- Time Cut: Have an elevator pitch
- Disengaged Executives: Do a process check
- Food Fight: Get help from your sponsor
- Decision Maker Leaves: Ask for a decision
- Topic Change: Confirm agenda/check with sponsor
- Side Talk: Politely re-engage
- Energetic Discussion: Don't miss anything

Creating Winning
Executive Presentations

W hat matters at the top level is the content of your presentation. It is not a time to try to be entertaining or charismatic. The audience is there to make decisions and is under pressure to move quickly through the agenda. If the homework has been done, and the content is relevant and delivered in a timely manner, your listeners will overlook poor presentation style.

On the other hand, no one told me that they preferred a bad speaker. When it comes to content vs. delivery, go for content. Now, C-level executives are humans who, like any other audience, will be influenced (unconsciously) by how the message is delivered. A speaker who mumbles, looks at the floor, does not seem enthusiastic, and reads PowerPoint slides will have an uphill battle. Imagine two presenters competing for funding with the exact same content. One has poor delivery; the other shows up with energy and passion. Guess who wins?

With all this as background, Part III takes you through the critical issues that can lead to a successful presentation: content development and delivery style. You will learn why you must be able to facilitate as well as speak; why you must make your "first line your bottom line," and why the dialogue is more critical than your visual aids. You will also learn the tricks of effective delivery. The executives don't want to see a lot of razzle-dazzle, but they do want to see a speaker with energy. After reading Part III, you'll have what it takes to win their hearts and their minds.

CHAPTER

11

Content + Facilitation + Listening + Improv = Success

Eighty percent of your success at the top level is your ability to facilitate the meeting. Only 20 percent is due to the content per se.

—Steve Kirsch

I don't care much about style. I care more about content, and I particularly care about the interaction in a presentation.

—Audrey MacLean

The extremely successful and effective people we have introduced to you in Part II as our heroes are really not different from mid-level managers in most companies. In training over 10,000 people on these skill sets, we have learned a lot about the challenges facing mid-level people. Some have hopes of moving up to the C-level, others are happy where they are. Some have well-developed presentation skills, many do not. Some can facilitate meetings well, others are only focused on their content. There is a huge variation. One thing that's consistent, though, is the thirst to learn the secrets of successful top-level presentations.

The biggest surprise for us has been how few people in the middle ranks know about these top-level communication skills. They know there is something very different at that level, but they're not sure what it is. Greg Fant, Chief Marketing Officer, One Kings Lane, said that he had been looking for MBA programs that taught this strategic approach to upward communication so his people would be better prepared. He found none. Greg observed, "A skill that was missing in these programs was related to communication skills required in less formal, 'small room' meetings with execs, i.e., the ability to deliver concise, thoughtful information with clarity in a tight time window. That falls into the bucket of having 'strong executive presence' — the area that often accelerates or slows an individual's rise in a given organization." *(See Chapter 2.)*

Preparation and Homework

Contrary to standard presentations which may require simply pulling together a few slides, top-level meetings require significant homework, which includes (but goes way beyond) your presentation content. "In the environment we're in today where things move quickly, where there's lots going on, and where everybody's multitasking and solving many problems at once — the more you can do your homework and align yourself with what the other person is worried about — the more successful you'll be," advised Ned Barnholt.

Failure to prepare for a C-level meeting hit Larry Lenox hard. In 1999, he was Senior Training and Development Manager at Cisco. He needed top-level support for a new workshop in their Executive Development Program. Larry got a valuable meeting with John Chambers, the CEO. As Larry unfolded his plans, Chambers agreed with him and wanted to move forward. Then Chambers said, "Have you checked with the people who will have to implement this plan?"

Larry said "No."

Chambers responded, "Well, you need to go check with them and get their buy-in before we can move forward." The meeting was over.

> If you walk into a room and want me to make a $10 million decision, but you haven't even talked to the person who is going to have to implement it, you can't possibly expect me to make that decision.
>
> —Ginger Graham

C-level executives are successful only through the support of the people they lead. Chambers was reluctant to support the program until he was confident the people who'd need to implement it also supported it. After Larry went back and got the buy-in, Chambers approved it.

As the CEO, Ginger Graham was very clear about the importance of this type of support, "If you've already talked to the people who'll be affected by your proposal, brought them into the discussion, surfaced their issues, and you all want me to make that decision, it's pretty easy for me to do."

Audience Analysis

A management team is just a collection of people, and you need to know these people—why they're there and what they're trying to get done—if you want to get decisions from them.

—Ginger Graham

With so much riding on it, a presenter should plan very carefully for that top-level presentation. Analyze the audience. What is their preference for qualitative versus quantitative information? Who can you meet with before the meeting? Who is likely to support your idea? Who will oppose it?

As Steve Blank says:

> There are typically three kinds of agendas: a status agenda, a decision agenda, and more than likely, a hidden agenda. With your butt on the line, you need to take these agendas quite seriously. It's up to you to understand what the people you're presenting to are about.

Steve Blank

Some of our senior executives learned that rule the hard way. John Kispert recalls his first presentation to senior management:

> 'That was the worst meeting I've been to in my entire life,' one of my early mentors told me afterwards. I was just shattered because I had spent the entire weekend preparing for it. I should have spent a lot more time with my management

team, finding out who I was talking to, why I was talking to them, and what they were looking for.

"You're not going to achieve your objectives unless you really fundamentally understand your audience and what they're trying to achieve," said Bryan Lamkin. Keep in mind that the important decisions are made prior to the meeting. Dan Warmenhoven observed that, "What happens *before* the meeting is more important than what happens *at* the meeting." When you walk into that room, you should already know who's with you and who opposes you.

> A good executive team doesn't let presenters just walk in the door without one of the executive team members having spent the time to understand the topic and to champion that topic to the executive staff.
>
> —Bryan Lamkin

Also remember that CEOs answer to many audiences: shareholders, analysts, employees, customers, management, even community groups. One minute they may be dealing with a Wall Street phone call, and the next minute making an employee video. While you charge into the presentation room feeling urgent about what you are presenting, keep in mind the executives' views span the entire business. They may be concerned with what happened in finance, manufacturing, or quality assurance moments before you got there.

Recall my presentation to Dick Anderson from Chapter 1. Had I been aware of the larger scope of his concerns that day, my meeting might have had a different outcome. Let the C-level executives know that you appreciate the huge scope of their responsibilities and their time constraints, and that you want to get right to the point. While the Krause and Keltner research indicates top-level people may be a little light in the empathy department, your ability to extend it to them will certainly not hurt your career.

Presentation Skills

Another huge gap in people's leadership skills is the ability to develop and deliver a tightly focused, impactful presentation. It is amazing to see someone who has been in a leadership role

for perhaps 10 years and may have several hundred people reporting to him or her but who still cannot present well. We see the symptoms of this problem all the time: no bottom line, over-reliance on PowerPoint, monotone delivery, and no audience interaction.

Our *Speaking Up®* training workshops make only a passing nod to presentations skills. We have always assumed mid-level people surely must have mastered these simple skills to get to the level they have. Not true. So now we'll turn our attention to how to be successful at the top level. If your professional tool kit needs an upgrade, taking classes in presentation skills, listening skills, and facilitation skills would be a great addition. Until then, here are some tips to tide you over.

Take the Bullet Now

There are three areas you need to master to present well at the top level: the people, the presentation, and improvisation. The people who have the right balance of these elements usually get what they came for. Here's an example:

Robert Drolet

The year was 1985. Army Colonel Robert Drolet was presenting at the Pentagon in front of four generals and Reagan appointee James R. Ambrose, Under Secretary of the Army. He recalled that when he got to his third slide,

> The Under Secretary started fiddling with papers on his desk. I looked up at him and said, 'Mr. Secretary, you've stopped listening, so there's no sense in me talking because you're not listening. You either don't like what I've said or you disagree with my briefing.' The generals almost died. He looked up at me and said, 'Colonel, you're right. I already know where you're going, I don't agree, and I want you to change what you are doing.'
>
> So I went back, re-did my study, came back two weeks later, and I was successful. You might as well find out what the rub is. You're going to fail anyway. Why waste 20 more minutes? Take the bullet now.

Drolet's story is a textbook example of what we call the "READ" strategy:

- He (R) "read" the room. He paid attention to how his audience was responding, especially the Under Secretary.
- He (E) "evaluated" the situation based on nonverbal input.
- He (A) "acknowledged" what was happening and asked for direction.
- He (D) "determined" the next steps, i.e., deciding to end his presentation and come back later after making the necessary changes.

While this may seem straightforward and simple, it takes a great deal of self-awareness, confidence, and skill. To manage this situation, Drolet used three overlapping skills: Facilitating, Listening, and Improvising. We've talked about all three in our hero stories. Now let's explore them in more detail.

Facilitation Skills

Steve Blank says you must be able to move from "presentation mode" into "process mode." Presentation mode is what you are talking *about*, while the process mode is *how* you are talking about it. If things are cruising along the way you'd planned—issues are being discussed, decisions are being made, and action items are being agreed to—then you may not need to pay much attention to "process." If, as Brent Bloom experienced (Chapter 6), things career off the track into conflict, loss of focus, distractions, etc., then it's time to take off your presentation hat, and put on your process hat. Failing to make this adjustment could damage your presentation and the outcome of the meeting.

Examples: Process Interventions

- You notice half the group is engaged in texting, reading emails, or talking on their phones, and the others' eyes are glazed over (Chapter 5). Process response: "Let me stop for a moment. It looks like I've lost the room. Is this still an important topic? Do you think we're moving in the right direction?"

- Suddenly the conversation turns confrontational with the executives attacking each other (Chapter 6). Process response (to your sponsor): "Dan, I'm concerned we're getting a bit off track. What should we do?" Note that your sponsor has the power to refocus the group; you don't.

- You notice that the key decision maker (let's say it is the CEO) gets up and heads for the door (Chapter 7). Process response: "Excuse me Ms. CEO, I see that you have to leave. Should I stop and wait for you to come back, or do you want me to continue?"

Facilitation skills are about your ability to sense when there has been a shift in the direction or tenor of the group. Noticing what has happened, you comment on it and take action to get things back on track. People lacking this skill will just keep blundering along with their slides, oblivious to the fact that they've "lost the room." They may also have lost the project, lost executive support, and maybe even lost their careers. Remember Bryan Lamkin's comment, "A presentation cannot make a career, but a presentation can undo a career."

As we saw with Julie Patel and Sharon Black, the key to a successful intervention is being able to "read the room" using your facilitation skills. At that point, listening skills and being able to improvise will help you win the day.

Listening Skills

Throughout his energetic discussion presentation (Chapter 10), Andy Billings demonstrated how listening is the foundation for the other skills and the backbone of successful meeting facilitation. It requires the listener, for a moment anyway, to slip out of his or her own skin and into the world of the speaker. It's harder than it sounds. For example, let's say you're presenting to your senior team and having a dialogue with the CFO.

Ineffective Way

CFO: "Your new delivery plan fails to take into account that oil is at $125 a barrel. That will seriously impact our margins."

You: "No, that will not be a problem. Our projections take into account oil fluctuation cost year over year."

So what is wrong with that response? Mainly, it rolls right over the CFO's profitability concern. Your position may be well thought out and researched, and may finally prove to be the correct solution, but with a snappy retort and one beginning with the confrontational tone, "No," the CFO will be on the defensive. You might get a response like:

CFO: "Hold on. With the Middle East in chaos, the old models are out the window. I simply won't approve this delivery plan. Go find an alternative and come back in two weeks."

It's unlikely that the CFO will tolerate being corrected in public by a subordinate. So your proposal takes a hit. More prep time. More meeting time. More delays. Meanwhile the competition is moving their product to market. That famous line from the movie "Cool Hand Luke" comes to mind: "What we have here is a failure to communicate."

Better Way: Active Listening

Active listening, a communication skill based on the work of psychologist Carl Rogers (Chapter 10, page 72), involves giving undivided attention to the speaker. With active listening, or paraphrasing, you reflect back to the speaker your understanding of his or her concerns, while checking that you've accurately understood what they've said. Here is how you might handle the CFO interaction using active listening:

> **CFO:** "Your new delivery plan fails to take into account that oil is at $125 a barrel. That will seriously impact our margins."

> **You:** "With our razor-thin margins on this new release, the higher gas prices could actually put us into the red. Is that it?"

> **CFO:** "Yes, exactly. We have to show improvements in our quarterly numbers or our stock price is going to take a swan dive." (Because you used an active listening response, the CFO now feels safe enough to reveal a deeper concern. Active listening helps to peel the emotional onion. This is good. The dialogue is still going.)

> **You:** "We're worried about the stock price too. Our major fuel supplier has guaranteed us that due to their reserves, they'll be able to keep our costs no higher than last year's rate. I'd be happy to send you the documentation. Would that help?"

> **CFO:** "Yes that might work. Please send it right away."

So here is an attitude of collaboration rather than confrontation. Listening well made the difference. The decision making process is moving forward. But, it is not easy.

So how do you listen well? As Rogers says, the goal is to "enter thoroughly, completely, and empathically into the other person's frame of reference." The CFO in our fictitious conversation is concerned about stock price, and maybe at a deeper level, her job. To gain her trust it is critical to let her know you can see things her way. It's human nature to trust people who seem to understand our concerns.

> A lot of actors act at you not with you. They don't listen. It's not just the words they miss, but they also miss the soul of the other actor.
>
> —Jack Lemmon

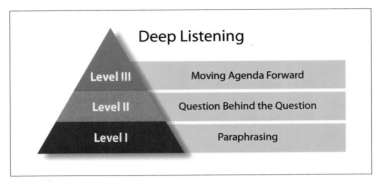

Figure 11.1 Deep Listening

About now, you may be thinking, "Oh, come on, listening skills in a tough-minded business environment? Really? No way! Too soft, even 'touchy-feely.'" The truth is just the opposite. Good listening can be critical in putting together profitable deals that bring new products to market. Steve Blank has found that listening actually moves the meeting forward. It is nothing less than a productivity tool. Before answering a tough board challenge or question, Steve may respond, "Let me make sure I understand what you just said." He then paraphrases his understanding of the question. This has two benefits: First, it clarifies the question so he knows he is answering the right question. Second, it gives him time to think.

Deep Listening

There are three levels of what I call "Deep Listening." (Figure 11.1)

Level I: Paraphrasing

This involves putting in your own words what the other person has said. This helps clarify the issue, and is especially good for a complicated or hostile question. It can immediately decrease the tension in an angry exchange.

Level II: Question Behind the Question

According to Dan Warmenhoven, the speaker who can answer not just the surface question, but also the question behind the question, is going to come across as "a much more compelling presenter." This is an extremely sophisticated response because it means the speaker really hears the underlying concerns and can acknowledge those in the answer in the heat of the moment.

Here's an example, courtesy of Melissa Schwartz, PowerSpeaking's VP of Training.

Question behind the Question

Eight years ago, when I was just 32, I was teaching a *Speaking Up®* workshop at one of our major clients in Silicon Valley. The room was full of gray-haired men. I was only five minutes into the welcome when a gentleman, with his arms crossed in front of him, said to me, "How old are you anyway?" I sensed anger in his voice, and knew I had to step back and respond to the question behind his question.

On the surface, the question was about my chronological age, but that wasn't the real issue. I sensed it was more about whether the day was going to be valuable for him. There was also emotion behind his question. Did I have the credibility and experience to be teaching him? Going a little deeper, perhaps he felt annoyed with the fact that his "teacher" was in the same age group as his children.

In order to diffuse his concern and move forward I needed to paraphrase and get at the underlying content and intent of his question. So I said, "You came to this class expecting to see someone who looks like an executive teaching it." (He nodded.) "But you got me instead." (He smiled.) "You might be wondering if today is going to be valuable for you and what my credentials are that qualify me to lead you through this content. Is that it?" To my surprise, with a smile on his face, he said "Yes." Now I could respond to his concern and move forward. I told him about the solid research supporting the program and how long I'd been teaching it. That seemed to satisfy him. So the question behind his question about my age was really about whether or not this day would be a waste of his time. (At the end of the day, he mentioned to me how valuable it had been.)

Level III: Moving the Agenda Forward

Steve Blank points out that the ultimate goal of good listening is to drive the meeting forward: "Here is what I heard, and I think that means this ... So do I have an agreement since we all believe this, that we can now move forward?" Here's another example using our CFO interaction from earlier:

> **Level I Paraphrasing:** "You're concerned about fuel costs, is that it?"
>
> **Level II Question behind the Question:** "Fuel costs can bring up more troubling issues about our stock price, and maybe even our future profitability."
>
> **Level III Moving the Agenda Forward:** "Since we agree that I'll get you the documentation on our vendor's commitment, are we ready to consider the next agenda item?"

Listening to Control or to Connect

According to Andy Billings:

> There are two ways to listen. You can listen to control, which means you are looking for the opportunity to jump in, to interrupt and steer that conversation, or conversely, you can listen to connect, which means you are genuinely trying
>
>
>
> to understand what the other person thinks and what his or her point of view is.
>
> People can sense the difference between whether you're trying to control them and move them through an agenda or whether you are listening to connect. By paraphrasing you communicate that you're trying to connect and trying to understand what's on his or her mind.

Improvisation

To risk is to lose your footing momentarily.
To not risk is to lose your self.

—Soren Kierkegaard
Philosopher

Improvisation is the final skill you will need in a fast-paced, high-stakes, senior-level meeting. When you've noticed there is a problem, and you've moved from presentation mode into process mode, you'll need to improvise. This is the 'D' in our R.E.A.D. strategy. You determine what to do and take action. When Colonel Robert Drolet "confronted" Under Secretary Ambrose, he took a huge risk, but he was ready to take Ambrose's direction. In other words, he was ready to improvise a new solution.

The Neurobiology of Improvisation

Recent brain research shows that people who can improvise are able to turn off the self-critical parts of the brain. Dr. Charles Limb, and his colleagues wired up jazz musicians inside an MRI scanner and had them improvise on a small keyboard they could play lying flat on their backs.

During improvisation, the prefrontal cortex, which is where the problem solving and "sense of self" reside, essentially turned off. Many other parts of the brain associated with creativity lit up while the musicians were improvising. The researchers suggest that creativity is thus a broad spectrum event in the brain.

Presenters who are able to turn off their slides, or "give up the middle part of the presentation," as Robert Drolet said, and go where the conversation leads them, are actually reconfiguring their brains. Presenters who cannot do this neurological gymnastics will not gain the trust of their C-level audiences.[1]

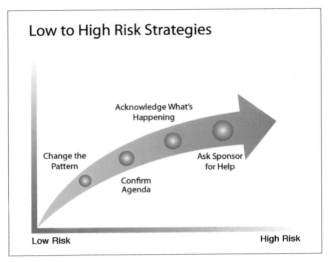

Figure 11.2 Risk Assessment Curve

When it comes to risk taking, you'll need to gauge the culture you're in. Corporations are different. Some want more compliance; some reward boldness. Most executives we've worked with are looking for people with courage. These are the people they want to give more responsibility to. Here is our "Risk Assessment Curve."(Fig. 11.2) Consider how gutsy or risk-averse you are and respond accordingly.

This is a variation on the old "elephant in the room" situation. You see that something is not right. You may not want to call attention to it. Maybe it will just go away. Unlikely. What to do? Depending on how comfortable you are with risk, or how tolerant the culture is for directness, you can make your decision.

At the low end of the spectrum, seeing that people have, for example, stopped listening, you might change the pattern by using the 'B' key on the computer to make the screen go blank and jolt the audience back to attentiveness. Slightly more risky is to verbally admit that, "I may have lost the room," followed by a reconfirmation of the value of the agenda. (See what Julie did with Disengaged Executives in Chapter 5.)

Taking this a bit further, you can identify what the problem is as Robert Drolet did when he stated, "You've stopped listen-

Rules of Improvisation

Jazz musician Dave Brubeck was asked if there are rules of improvisation. He said "Absolutely. If you get them wrong you won't be invited to play with those musicians ever again."*

ing." Finally, a direct request for help from your sponsor to get things back on track may be an admission that you need major help from the only person in the room with the authority to get the group refocused.

Let's take a closer look at how you can make the best use of your sponsor.

Role of the Sponsor

Mid-level presenters are smart and accomplished business people. If they're invited to address the most senior leadership in the company, it's because they have something important to contribute. But as much as a mid-level person might yearn for top-level exposure, getting in front of that meeting is "by invitation only." This is where the sponsor comes in.

The person who arranges for the presentation (the sponsor) thinks the topic is important enough that it should be given

---

* *In His Own Sweet Way,* Brubeck documentary shown at the Monterey Jazz Festival, 2011. In a striking parallel to business, it is not clear what the rules are, but the novice better learn them if he or she wants to move on.

precious time on the senior-level agenda (Remember this is costing the corporation at least $30,000 an hour.) Furthermore, the sponsor has faith that the presenter is up to the challenge of speaking well for the project in question, and representing the functional area effectively.

The sponsor is a critical lynchpin for success before, during, and after the meeting. Before the meeting your sponsor can help you plan your overall meeting strategy. Your sponsor will be able to bring you up to speed on the politics in the room and help you plan how to handle problems if the meeting veers off track.

You and your sponsor should plan for possible "off track" scenarios before the meeting. For example, if a food fight breaks out, or suddenly they want to take the meeting in a completely new direction like what happened to Brent and Julie (Chapters 6 and 7), your sponsor has the authority to refocus the group, whereas it could be inappropriate for you to do that. After the meeting, you can check in with your sponsor for critical feedback on what worked and what needs improvement in your presentation. In addition, he or she can help you with the next steps after the meeting.

As Steve Blank pointed out, there may also be a "virtual sponsor" in the room. This person is higher up in the same functional area as the presenter. Steve advises, "Make sure the virtual sponsor has a copy of what you are about to present in advance. You don't want the virtual sponsor to be surprised and perhaps fail to support your proposal."

Ginger Graham was even more emphatic about lining up allies: "You cannot afford to go into a room full of politics without full functional support because you know the other side is opposed merely by the presence of what part of the company you came from." She added, "So if you're from sales and marketing, you need to make sure that the vice president of marketing—and maybe even the president of the sales organization—are also aligned with your position."

> Think about the culture and how decisions get made. Find who can help champion your idea and be a mentor for you through the process of getting your idea sold or accepted.
>
> —Ned Barnholt

Use a Coach

While your sponsor is the person who gets you on the agenda and can help you during the meeting, a coach can give you a roadmap. Coaches can tell you what to expect from the C-level group because they've been there before. In addition to giving you cues about the political realities you're about to confront, they can tell you what questions may come up, and what kind of distractions to expect like food fights, topic change, or time cut.

Use that information to go through your presentation out loud with a partner. It will prepare you for whatever happens. Harold Fethe commented, "It's amazing how much adrenalin and how much of a genuine reaction you can get even though it's just a practice partner peppering you with tough questions."

Do a Dry Run

Once you've prepared, be sure to have that all-important "dry run" with your sponsor or the most senior person in your functional area who will be in the meeting. A dry run will give you an even better feel of what it will be like, and will allow you to practice handling tough questions or difficult group interactions with someone who knows the drill.

That helped Dan Warmenhoven when he was starting out:

> I was an engineering manager for one of the many product programs at IBM. I had to make a report to the executive committee. I'd never done anything like that before. It was a little intimidating. There were seven layers of management between me and the people I was presenting to, and numerous reviews along the way.
>
> When the big day came, the structure had been reworked two or three times. Everyone had contributed something to the message. So by the time we got there, it was a well-polished presentation. It went very well.

Throw You Under the Bus?

Audrey MacLean pointed out that the top people in your silo should be invested enough in your success to spend at least

30 minutes reviewing your presentation. If they are unwilling to take the time, then "...you should wonder if they are going to throw you under the bus." She went on. "If they aren't interested in you being a success then they may be using your presentation as a trial balloon."

Audrey MacLean

Summary

As we've explored in this chapter, the skills of facilitation, listening, and improvisation are key to keeping an executive audience engaged during a fast-paced, top-level meeting.

In addition, a lot of preparation will mean the difference between success and failure:

- Do extensive homework on who will be there
- Use a coach
- Do a dry run
- Coordinate with your sponsor before, during, and after the meeting
- Keep your virtual sponsor in the loop

As you can see, there is a lot to consider before you put your presentation together. Now that you have the big picture, in the next chapter we'll show you a system for developing and delivering your presentation that will get your point across clearly while keeping them focused.

12

Public Speaking Unplugged

I sit through so damn many of these executive presentations. It is painful. There are two times when you are alone in life: one is when you die, and the other is when you present to senior management.

—Rick Wallace

As we've seen, C-level executives are very bright people living in high-stress, demanding environments with little job security and not much support. They can be abrupt and hard to please. Due to a "perfect storm" of personality variables, performance pressure, and environmental factors, top-level people are a very tough audience. Additionally, putting them in a room for a presentation costs the shareholders a lot of money. This is made even worse by the fact that more than half of the presentations they see are total failures. All this paints a dismal and scary picture for the aspiring presenter.

But wait! There's hope.

First of all, let's remember that the executives want you to do well. It is in the best interest of the company to have successful, informative presentations. Ned Barnholt advised, "They are not a bunch of wolves sitting around the table, but people just like you who are interested in what you have to say." That goes a long way toward creating the right environment for a successful discussion. Secondly, they've told us what works. This is not rocket science. It's very learnable. So let's find out how to create a winning presentation.

Oracle VP Markus Zirn commented that at the top level, your presentations don't need, in fact, better not have, a bunch

Markus Zirn

of bells and whistles. Senior people want the information fast, clear, and concise so that they can make a decision and move on. Zirn calls it being "unplugged." It's an excellent metaphor. When you go up to the C-suite, forget everything you ever learned about public speaking (well, almost everything).

You've probably heard all the advice about public speaking: Open with something shocking and memorable, have strong eye contact, use big gestures, use stories, use strong vocal projection, etc., etc. Good advice. In fact, we teach a lot of this in our PowerSpeaking® and HighTechSpeaking® workshops. However, when you're a guest at a time-pressured, top-level decision meeting, this advice, which works so well at lower levels, could be a career killer with senior executives.

Because of this unique audience, things like content, delivery, and audience involvement are handled differently than in standard presentations. Table 12.1 compares the characteristics of the different business presentations.

So, if the standard approach isn't recommended, what do you do instead? Answer: develop a new strategy consisting of three things: The People, The Presentation, and Improvisation.

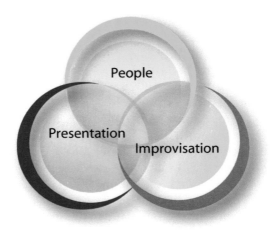

Speaking Up®: Surviving Executive Presentations fits into a larger framework of typical business presentations. While my focus in this book is on top-level presentations (perhaps better called "discussions"), many of the skills are drawn from other types of business presentations as well.

Types of Business Presentations

Type	Audience	Audience Focus	Visual Aids	Stories vs Data	Emotion vs Logic	Humor	Timing	Audience Participation
Speech	Community, associations / professional groups	Moderate	Rare	Heavy stories	More emotion	Yes	Short: 20 min.	Little
Standard Internal Presentation	Management peers, subordinates	Low to moderate	Heavy	Stories and data	Emotion and logic	Maybe	Long: 45 - 60 min.	Some
Senior Executive Presentation	Senior executives	High focus and engagement	Few	Data	Logic	Dangerous	Variable, Usually short Time gets cut	Very heavy discussion

Table 12.1 Types of Business Presentations

Senior Executive Presentations Are Different!

DAY TO DAY PRESENTATIONS	SENIOR EXECUTIVE PRESENTATIONS
The People	**The People**
• Audience of ordinary people	• Audience of time-pressured Type 'A' drivers
• Audience has no power over you	• Audience can fire or promote you
The Presentation	**The Presentation**
• You set the time and other parameters	• They set and / or cut your time at will
• Stories and self-disclosure valued	• Stories and self-disclosure dangerous
• Opening up to you	• Make your first line your bottom line
• Handouts at the beginning	• Handouts at the end
• Content up to you	• Content tightly connected to company's financial success
• You put Q&A at the end if you prefer	• Q&A happens from the start
• Can tolerate, though may not like long PPT presentations	• Will not tolerate long PPT presentations
• On your own for rehearsal and content review	• Use other senior mentors and coaches to help review content and to rehearse
The Process	**The Process**
• Process concerns rarely matter	• Ability to understand and use process critical
• You are in charge	• You are not in charge
• You are the main event	• You are a guest at their meeting
• May not need interaction	• Interaction highly prized
• It is a presentation	• It is a "framed discussion"
• Timing may be loose	• Time constrained environment
• Controlling audience problems is your job	• Controlling audience problems is their job

Table 12.2 Senior Executive Presentations Are Different!

Table 12.2 pinpoints some of the key differences between standard and top-level presentations.

Now let's look at the basic structure of the presentation itself so that the next presentation you prepare will almost write itself.

The Framework

Based on executive feedback, here is a model that will work every time. This presentation outline can help you be concise, support your "ask" with data, and close with clear action steps. Your presentation will resonate with senior people if you follow this model. The framework (Figure 12.1) will also help you prepare quickly and efficiently.

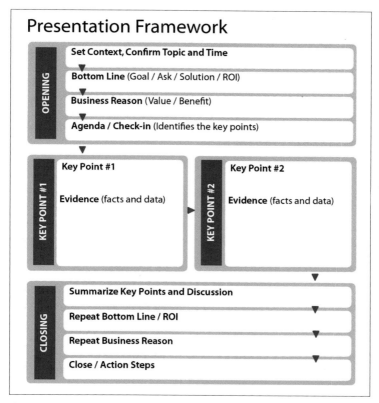

Figure 12.1 Presentation Framework

(This framework can be downloaded from our web page: *http://www.powerspeaking.com/files/pdf/SEP_Framework.pdf.*)

The Opening: Set the Context
"Why are we here?"

Begin by confirming the topic and the time. Clarify why this meeting has been scheduled, what you are discussing, and how much time you've got. SalesForce.com SVP Linda Crawford told us, "My days are fully booked. Because of my role, I can meet on 10 vastly different topics in a day. To make the time productive for me and for you, the first thing for you to do is reconfirm the topic we are discussing and the outcomes that you want."

First Line, Bottom Line/Get to the Point!

*Be concise. I don't have the bandwidth or
the time.*

—John Kispert

*Nobody has ever told me that I've given a
presentation that's too short.*

—Corrine Nevinny

Your top-level audience is simply the most demanding audience you will ever face.[1] You are dealing with a room full of very bright, Type 'A' personalities. Their routes to the C-level were through line positions that are directly related to the bottom-line success of the company. They want to get down to business, especially since according to the May, 2007 *Harvard Business Review*,[2] their futures rest on the quarterly stock price.

They want the recommendations at the beginning and they want you to support your recommendations with data, not with stories. The dozens of C-level executives we've interviewed, from large companies and small, from high-tech to biotech to no tech, and from a member of the United States Congress, have the same message: Get to the point. "You can hold off telling me what you want, and start by giving me data, data, data and I'll start poking holes in your data because I don't know where you're trying to take me," said Ginger Graham. "But if you tell me up front where you're trying to go, I can listen in the places that I think matter as opposed to challenging you about everything."

Doris Engibous agrees, "I like to know the bottom line first. I like people to give me the answer then peel it back. I don't like long-winded tee ups."

Steve Blank actually had to tell a brilliant business development manager that his future employment at the company was contingent on his learning how to get to the point. Steve recalls:

> He loved to tell stories. And we'd start with the weather and his trip and what he had for breakfast, and meanwhile I couldn't tell whether the building was on fire, or we had just raised $10 million, or he had a great breakfast. As the CEO of a start-up, I'm constantly bombarded with lots of decisions to make. I'm processing not only the person I'm looking at,

but I'm dealing with 50 other inputs—and that's in the last hour. So I just need the main facts about why we're having this meeting.

Although this book focuses on speaking to decision makers in Fortune 500 companies, the demands described here are by no means confined to them. If you work for a non-profit—the arts, academia, government agencies, or the helping professions—you'll find similar expectations in people at the top of your organization. An artistic director of a theater company or symphony orchestra, an administrator of a clinic, or a chairman of an academic department can be every bit as demanding as a CEO, even though they don't play in the same financial leagues.

Anna Eshoo

For example, Congresswoman Anna Eshoo expressed how exasperating it is to have constituents schedule a meeting with her and not be able to get to the point:

Some people feel they need to tell me everything about themselves, so I'll know how important they are. They have to tell a story, so they start out with Adam and Eve, and then finally get to the 21st Century. I don't have time for it. Get to the point! In Washington, you never know when the bells are going to go off. When the bell rings, I have exactly fifteen minutes to get to the Capitol and vote. I'm not going to miss a vote because someone doesn't know how to get to the point.

I want them to feel comfortable, but they go on and on and on. I feel embarrassed for them. As the kids say, TMI: too much information. There were people that came today, and I said six or seven times in half an hour, "How is it that you think I can help you?" They couldn't get to the point.

All of this also applies internationally. For example, MBA student Bhatupe Mhango who presents to Secretaries General at the United Nations—people like Kofi Annan—confirmed, "They demand that you get to the point immediately. They just don't have time to waste. It is just like the Fortune 500 C-levels in your study."

> The best structural presentations I've seen always start off with what I need from you (why am I here, basically), what's the problem or topic, what's the proposed solution. Then comes all the rationale and supporting documentation. We want to know your bottom line first so we can understand the derivation of the rest of your presentation.
>
> —Dan Warmenhoven

> Start with your punch line at the beginning.
>
> —Steve Kirsch

> Net it out up front. Net it out at the end.
>
> —Bryan Lamkin

> It is a waste of time to come in and not get your point across quickly.
>
> —John Kispert

Bottom Line

Once the purpose, context, and anticipated length of the meeting are clear, state plainly what your goals are for the meeting. Are you asking for head count? Approval? Budget? In stating your "First Line, Bottom Line," make it short, and crisp, e.g.,  "Today I am requesting $10M* for our new marketing plan for Asia for this fiscal year." This saves time, and lets them know where you are headed, right up front.

You've Got 30 Seconds

"You have 30 seconds to get to the point," according to Steve Blank. He explained, "In the past few years, smartphones have

---

* In reality, a large dollar amount request would have been discussed with the executive stakeholders before the meeting. You would have a good sense of the outcome of the meeting beforehand.

gotten so good that I now have in front of me a telephone, the Internet, a computer, a video camera, and all my email. If you don't get right to the point, I'm gone."

Avoid the Snoring

Dan Eilers advised, "Put your conclusion up front." Once when Dan failed to do that early in his career, two members of Apple's board of directors started to snore before he had wrapped up. To his chagrin, they never heard his "call to action."

Starting with the "ask" may be particularly hard for those who've had technical training. For example, we worked with a group of engineers from a biotech company who organized their presentations to management like a technical journal article: hypothesis, experimental design, data collection and analysis, and lastly, the conclusions. They weren't getting traction from these presentations. After one day of *Speaking Up*® they flipped the "upside down" pyramid right side up. (Figure 12.2) That forced them to begin with the conclusion. They switched from the all too familiar "data dump" model to the "executive" model. While this initially felt unnatural and awkward, senior management loved it, and they started getting what they wanted.

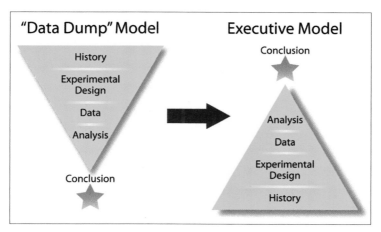

Figure 12.2 Data Dump vs. Executive Model

Return on Investment (ROI)

C-level executives hear requests like yours all the time. You are competing for a limited pool of money to fund many important projects. How are you going to make your request stand out from the others? One way is to calculate the ROI and put it up front.

> The bottom line statement you start with has to include all the key metrics: what's the investment, what's the return?
>
> —Dan Warmenhoven

> I always think: 'How does this effect the bottom line? Is this going to grow our business? Are we going to get more hits to our website?' You know, metrics that people can hold onto.
>
> —Corinne Nevinny

People are surprisingly resistant to including the ROI numbers, yet that is exactly what the executives want. It shows them you've done the hard thinking about what return they'll get on their investment.

Timing:
The "10/30 Rule"

The "10/30 Rule," which we saw violated in the Time Cut presentation in Chapter 4, says that if you are given 30 minutes on the agenda, prepare just 10 minutes of material. The executives will take the other 20 minutes for discussion and debate.

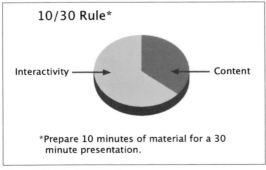

Figure 12.3 The 10/30 Rule

Dan Warmenhoven reinforced the point, "If you've got a half-hour on the agenda, you're not going to get through a half-hour presentation because we're not going to let you." Dan elaborated:

> Keep in mind you're a guest at their meeting, and they want plenty of time to discuss the issues. A successful meeting will mean that they talk more than you do. If they're discussing the merits of the ideas in your presentation rather than just listening to your rehearsed script, then you know they're interested. You'll probably fail if you bombard them with information they don't need or deny them the opportunity to debate the issue.
>
> The presenters who don't do well are those who are so rehearsed that they go from beginning to end with no air time for anybody in the audience. You actually lose your audience if you don't allow them to get their questions resolved in the flow. Interaction is essential. It's not a presentation; it's a framed discussion.

"If you want executives to really be part of your deal, you've got to engage them," Dan Eilers said. But you have to engage them quickly. Executives are under unrelenting time pressure. Successful presenters will get to the point immediately, are prepared for two-thirds of their time to be taken up with discussion, and also are prepared to have their time cut. Steve Bene, SVP and General Counsel for Electronic Arts, commented that executives find it a most welcome gift when a presenter says, "I can end early. Here, let me give you half of your time back."

The Body: Key Points—The Big Seven

Key points are the heart of your presentation. They are where you make your logical arguments. Key points at a senior meeting will be supported by data—well scrubbed data. Check and recheck the numbers. Top leaders are very numerate, so the data needs to be tight. As Harold Fethe reminds us, "Executives can do math on the fly just for the fun of it, and that is just what they do when they get bored in a meeting."

Topics, First Line, Bottom Line, and key points can cover a wide range, but certain problems and solutions consistently

Figure 12.4 The Big Seven

populate middle-management presentations. Executives worry about how to:

- Increase customer retention/attraction
- Increase efficiency/streamline processes
- Increase market share
- Increase profit/revenue (top concern)[3]
- Decrease cost/risk
- Decrease time to market

If your presentations relate to one of these issues, you will be speaking their language.

Accommodating Different Processing Styles

C-level executives understand that their audiences—customers, shareholders, employees, or Wall Street analysts—all have different processing styles. Reflecting on his executive team, Dan Warmenhoven observed that, "When it comes to absorbing information, they each do it in a different way. Some like humor, some just want to get focused." Ned Barnholt suggests, "Some of my audiences want it abstract, some want concrete data. Being prepared either way is important."

These executives move easily from one format to another. Steve Blank commented:

> At times I've presented the same data in four different formats. For the numbers people, I've done a spreadsheet. For the big-picture people, I've used bar charts and diagrams. If I'd had time, I would have done an animation of little bags of money moving from the customer into the company. That would have gotten everybody.

Similarly, Mark Leslie gauges the technical depth of his presentations depending on audience preferences:

> When I'm presenting to C-level people, I learn enough about them in advance to tailor my comments. If they like technical information, then I'll have a more technical orientation. If they are people who don't get that stuff, then I'll talk at a very high level and discuss big-picture ideas.

The Whole Brain® research of the late Ned Herrmann and his daughter, Ann Herrmann-Nehdi sheds light on what we're seeing here. Their Whole Brain® Model reflects 30 years of research on the four thinking styles: A–Analyzer; B–Organizer; C–Personalizer; D–Visualizer. Most people have a preference for one of these styles over the others. Some people have preferences for at least two styles.

Figure 12.5 Different Processing Styles

According to their research, only three percent of the population has a natural preference for thinking and approaching work from all four quadrants. Herrmann says, "Our international database clearly shows that the typical CEO is 'multi-dominant' and has usually three, and often four, strong primary preferences and therefore has a wider array of thinking options. As an occupational category, CEOs have four times the number of four-quadrant-balanced profiles."[4]

Ann Herrmann-Nehdi says the job of the CEO is to integrate all the different thinking styles on his or her C-level team. This research may give us a clue about why it seems so effortless for these executives to adapt to the audiences sitting in front of them. It may also be one of the key skills that gets them to the top of their companies.

When preparing your presentation, especially the body or the key points, think about different ways you could present the same information: bar charts; pie charts; a spreadsheet; photographs, and perhaps a summary using a short customer story. By presenting the same data in different ways, you can hit all the disparate processing styles in the room. As one executive put it, "When I presented the raw data, one group lit up. When I presented the charts, another group lit up. Finally, when I related the customer story, the last group lit up."

Presenting Bad News

If you have bad news, you better get it out in the open, and get it out real quick. The last thing you want is for me to figure it out before you tell me.

—John Kispert

Let the good news take the stairs, but make sure the bad news takes the elevator.

—N.R. Narayana Murthy
Harvard Business Review,
November, 2011

No one likes bad news, especially not when financial or legal problems could be involved. How you communicate the bad news is critical.

Brenda Rhodes shared how she dealt with just such a situation:

We were facing a terrible last quarter. I had to tell the investment community that we had stock that was under extreme pressure, that we had just finished a quarter that had very disappointing earnings, and that we had not finished negotiating our new credit line with the bank. I had to be honest and direct about it.

Brenda Rhodes

I went to that earnings call expecting that after I told them this bad news, the stock was going to drop like a rock again. I was shocked at the response. Not only did the stock not drop, we got messages saying, 'I went into the meeting thinking I was going to get rid of my position and then determined to keep it.' You can't move to solutions if you pretend like there's no problem.

In the event you have bad news to present, the executives were in complete agreement. There are four steps:

- Get the bad news out right away
- Explain why it happened
- Follow up with what you are planning to do to fix it
- Offer several solutions and let them choose

Confidently presenting a well thought out recovery plan and action steps is key. Fran Townsend, former White House Homeland Security Adviser, is blunt, "My job is to focus on the threats and the things that are not resolved. You never deliver bad news without the next sentence being what you're doing about it."

Don't bring me your problems. I want solutions.

—Rick Wallace

Rule of Three

Executives like choices. As you construct your presentation think of alternatives to what you are proposing. Give them some options. We've heard again and again that three seems to be the right number of choices. Let's say you are recommending solution 'C.' Present solutions 'A' and 'B' then describe why 'C' may be the better choice. Always let them know there are other options.

Paradoxically, recent research in persuasion[5] shows that arguing against your own recommendation will likely generate more support for what you want to do. It shows that you've done the hard thinking about the issues. It's disarming because you bring up potential objections before they do.

Stories vs. Data

Rule #1: Research shows that stories are far more effective than data for getting attention and increasing retention.[6]

Rule #2: Not at the C-level.

Robert Drolet

As we've seen, because of the pressure of time most executives do not find stories helpful in decision meetings. Robert Drolet is very clear on this:

> Decision briefings are serious. Decisions must be made that involve money, involve people, and involve resources. I wouldn't walk into a meeting with the Chief of Staff of the United States Army or the CEO of Lockheed Martin and start telling them a funny story: 'Guess what happened on the airplane flying in . . . ha ha.'

Time is a critical asset that has to be managed. These executives didn't come into that room to listen to a five-minute story from you. They came in to make a decision and leave because they have an agenda for that day they can't possibly meet.

Tolerance for stories will vary among companies and among executives, but generally you'll be more effective sticking with data. As Jane Shaw quipped, "In God we trust. Everybody else bring data." If you do use stories, make sure they are short and get right to the point.

Jane Shaw

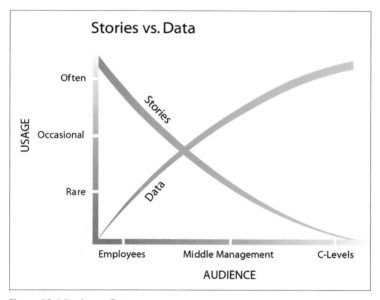

Figure 12.6 Stories vs. Data.

The Closing

The closing reflects the opening. First of all, summarize the key points and whatever discussion was generated. Next, repeat your First Line, Bottom Line and review the reasons you believe this is something the company should do. The most important part of the conclusion is the action steps.

You want clarity about what has happened as a result of your presentation and what commitments have been made. Have they approved your proposal? Have they agreed to support it? Have they allocated the money to make it happen? Perhaps they are not ready to make a decision for whatever reason—not enough information, timeframe doesn't work, conflicting projects, budget restraints, etc. Whatever the reason, the last part of your presentation should make it clear what the next steps are.

Follow-Up

Andy Billings recommends building in a cushion of time right after the meeting to reflect on what was said and what was committed to. He then emails everyone in the meeting for confirmation about what was agreed to. Sharon Black confirmed the importance of pulling together additional information and either going back to the next meeting herself, or giving her sponsor the necessary information and letting him go back for final approval. Brent Bloom added that a debriefing with his sponsor is always critical to discuss what he could have done better or differently in the meeting.

In summary, make sure that your presentations end with clarity about the next steps, then follow up with an email to confirm what needs to be done.

Be in the Top One Percent

Steve Kirsh

Want your next presentation to be successful? Steve Kirsch advised: You will be ahead of 99 percent of other presenters if you do just three things:

1. Tell me what you want in the first 30 seconds.

2. Tell me why it is important.

3. Get a commitment for the follow-up steps.

Remember Make It Collaborative

Dan Warmenhoven sees the collaborative attitude as central to effective top-level presentations:

> There are two ways to start a conversation when you walk into a room of executives. One is, 'It's us and them.' The other is a team approach, a discussion, as opposed to a presentation. If you get to the discussion stage, you'll find the collaboration happens very quickly, because the natural tendency on the part of the executive audience is to become very participative.

Karen Sage is clear about the presenter's role:

> The CEO's team is a club that you are not a member of, and you should not try to act like you are. You have to balance your lack of being a part of this club with independent confidence in yourself and what you have to offer. This is not the time to be overly familiar in your approach.

Summary

The *Speaking Up*® Framework gives you a fast and effective way to prepare. It has been well-tested. Use it to give your presentations structure, and to save preparation time.

Key takeaways:
- Start with a confirmation of time and topic
- State your "First Line, Bottom Line" and ROI
- Provide reasons for your "ask"
- Review the agenda
- Introduce key points and supporting data
- Expect dialogue and discussion
- Wrap up with a summary and a restatement of your "First Line, Bottom Line"
- Agree on next steps
- Use data rather than stories
- Follow up with key decision makers
- Remember, it's a discussion rather than a presentation

Now let's look at your delivery style.

13

Delivery Style

*Don't make yourself the lead
actor in this play. You're not.
Go in there and quickly, con-
cisely deliver the information,
answer questions, survive it,
and get out.*

George Gleeson

—George Gleeson, Regional Sales Manager,
Enterprise Hardware, Oracle

W hen you deliver your "New Employee Orientation" or
your "All Hands Meeting," strong style is
a must. You can even be charismatic. However,
when you hit the C-level, the executives are
just interested in getting business done, and
are less interested in charisma. It's not about
how you deliver your proposal, but rather
about the proposal itself.

Ned Barnholt reported seeing a particularly poor presenter who simply turned to the screen and read his slides to

senior management at Agilent.
"Content-wise it was a very
interesting idea, and I'm willing
to overlook the shortcomings
of the presentation in order to
focus on this opportunity."

Now let's be clear, executives
do not want a poor presenter.
What they do want is excellent
content—and oh, by the way,
if the presenter is also a good

Ned Barnholt

speaker, that is a real plus. If your style needs an upgrade, a good place to start is with our Style Hierarchy.

> Style is like icing on the cake. You can have lousy style, but if you have good content, you'll still be successful.
>
> —Robert Drolet

Style 101: Signal-to-Noise Ratio

> Content without style goes unnoticed, and style without content has no meaning.
>
> —Michael Alley
> Professor of Mechanical Engineering,
> Penn State

The "Style Hierarchy" is a way to conceptualize "The Big Seven" of style. In person, stand-up presentations to any group will involve all of these behaviors. The question is, "How aware are you of what you are doing in each area?"

While executives are most interested in your content, if you have poor delivery, it will make it harder for them to be persuaded by what you are saying. A speaker who mumbles, paces, fidgets, talks in a monotone, talks too fast without pauses, and won't make eye contact with the audience is seen as nervous and just not believable.

The question is, are you conscious of what you are doing with your body as you deliver your message? Most speakers are completely clueless about the physical part of their delivery. They are too nervous to think about it. When people get nervous, the fidgeting and hand wringing start up, and boom! There goes the value of the message.

The good news is that fixing this is easy. If your style needs a tune-up, take a class. Make sure the class includes video feedback and private coaching. You will improve your skills in no time. But, keep in mind, your content matters more than your delivery. The main reason to polish up your delivery is so people can hear your message more clearly.

Figure 13.1 Style Hierarchy

Classroom

Coaching

Think of a rocket putting a satellite into orbit. The rocket provides the thrust and power, but it is only the vehicle. What is important is the satellite. Same thing with your presentation. It is the message that counts. But your style is what puts it "in orbit." Or, borrowing from electrical engineering, the concept of "signal-to-noise ratio" is helpful here. Think of a radio with static. You are interested in the music, not the static. A strong signal will deliver the music. A weak signal will have a lot of distracting static. So, too, with your presentations. A weak presenter who may have great content, but is plagued with nervous mannerisms, will not get his or her message across. The strength of the signal is ruined because of the noise of the poor style. Put another way, poor delivery style can ruin good data!

Until you can take a video-based class, here is a crash course on style.

Eye Contact

When I was a senior in high school, my speech teacher, Mr. Ellers, told us, "Look above their heads. It will make you too nervous to look in their eyes." Or a variation on that, "Look at their forehead." Or, "Look at the back wall." Or, my personal favorite, "Imagine the audience in their underwear." Now, how that will make you feel more relaxed is beyond me. In fact, it could make you forget your content altogether. Of course, it's all total nonsense.

To connect with people and drive home your message, you need to look them squarely in the eyes. Select people randomly around the room. Hold eye contact with one person for a complete thought, then move on.

Eye contact

The meaning of eye contact, though, can have various cultural connotations. In Western cultures, eye contact is a sign of confidence and credibility, while in some other cultures it can be a sign of disrespect, or even of challenge. In some Japanese business cultures, for example, senior leaders will listen to a presenter with their eyes closed which says, "We trust what you are saying," or, "We are listening carefully to what you are saying." If you did not know this, it could be very disconcerting.

Facial Animation

By the time you get far enough up the chain to be addressing a senior-leadership meeting, you are undoubtedly enthusiastic about what you are presenting. Executives told us again and

Facial animation

again, they want to see that enthusiasm, but not a lot of rah-rah. Use your face to communicate your excitement about your topic. Don't be afraid to be animated: eyebrows up for good news as you are smiling, and the furrowed brow for serious issues, etc.

Pause

As if trying desperately to end this torture as soon as possible, nervous speakers talk too fast and never pause. On the other hand, speakers eager to connect with their audiences will use pauses to let their ideas sink in. The pause is often accompanied by longer eye contact and the holding of a gesture. Pauses under two seconds don't register. Three to four seconds, and it really hits home. Nine or ten seconds, they call 911.

Vocal Variety

Sergeant Friday from the old Dragnet TV show used to advise hysterical witnesses, "Just the facts ma'am. Just the facts," always in a total monotone. We see too many speakers who are doing their best imitation of Joe Friday. They think they

should present "just the facts" in a boring monotone. They mistakenly think the monotone increases their credibility, and that enthusiasm decreases their believability. Just the opposite is true. Recent research from MIT indicates that, in fact, vocal variety and animation increase rather than decrease your credibility.

Joe Friday
Photo courtesy Moviecraft, Inc.

In studies conducted at the Sloan School of Management at MIT, Professor Alex Pentland and his team found that the most persuasive people use a lot of vocal variety in their communications. This study received the "Best Idea of the Year" award from the *Harvard Business Review*.[1] So work on developing vocal delivery marked by highs and lows. Your audience will stay tuned in, and you'll be more credible. Say "Goodbye" to Sergeant Friday.

Believe it or not, your facial expression affects your voice. To make your voice sound brighter and more inviting, try smiling as you speak. Conversely, it is very hard to sound cheerful when you are frowning.

Gestures

Nervous speakers, if they gesture at all, often keep their hands clasped in front of their bodies, as though protecting them-

selves. It says to the audience, "I'm not sure of myself." It makes the audience doubt the speaker's confidence and credibility. Confident, persuasive speakers use bold gestures. They take up space and seem to be comfortable in their own skin. Use gestures effectively and your audience will not even be aware of your gestures. They will, however, be aware of how congruent you are with your message. Effective

Nervous gesture

style is invisible. It's a total package. (Pentland's MIT research confirms that animation increases believability.)

Rule of thumb: when gesturing, bring your hands up above your waist and out away from your body. While using both hands, or what we call "bilateral gestures," can look good, what looks even better is what we call "unilateral gestures,"

Bilateral gesture   **Unilateral gesture**

meaning that one hand gestures while the other is relaxed at your side or in your pocket.

Gestures are one of your most powerful communication tools. Use them to help your audience get the meaning visually of what your words are saying. Be descriptive. For example, to show sales growth, move your hand "up and to the right." In essence, to look and feel confident, let your hands and arms reflect what your words are saying.

The Pocket Myth

Speaking of pockets, you may have heard that you should never put your hands in your pockets. Again, my high school

speech teacher, dear old Mr. Ellers, used to admonish students that hands in the pockets made them "look too casual." With all due respect to Mr. Ellers, that is just not a problem. In fact it is an asset. Notice how often in the media you will see a relaxed, confident speaker with one hand in the pocket. It does indeed make you look casual, and guess what? That is just how effective speakers feel in front of the room. If the speaker looks relaxed and not nervous, the audience gets a sense of the speaker's confidence and hence, believability.

Use of the pocket

Movement

You will see nervous speakers either pacing back and forth in front of the room, or just the opposite, standing rigidly in one spot like a lamp post. Moving naturally with the flow of your content says nonverbally that you are relaxed and confident, and that you want to connect with people in different parts of the room.

Let your content guide your movement. You might, for example, set up your First Line, Bottom Line, ROI, and agenda in the center of the room, then move to the right to develop

3rd position

Stance disaster

Solid stance

your first key point, to the left for your second key point, and finally back to the center for your conclusion. Just be sure to avoid looking like a caged tiger or a statue.

Stance

Stance is at the bottom of our "Style Hierarchy" because it is the foundation of strong delivery. Nervous speakers demonstrate all manner of odd stances: shifting from one foot to the other, rocking back on one heel, rocking up on one foot, or my favorite—left over from childhood ballet lessons—the dreaded "third position," where the feet are held close together with one pointing out at a 90-degree angle to the other. This is often accompanied by a high voice and hands clasped tightly in front of the body. A stance like this says, "Don't take me seriously."

A more credible stance is like a solid athletic stance. Feet are about hip-width apart, firmly connected to the floor, and pointed straight ahead. When the speaker moves to one side or the other, the feet are replanted in the new position.

Don't Sit at the Table!

During the video production of *Speaking Up*®, we were surprised at the strength of the executives' negative reactions when Sharon Black sat at the table to make her presentation. They felt she had violated their space. One executive commented, "Seats at the table are for the senior-leadership team. The presenter should stand at the front of the table, not sit."

Visual Aids

It's like having clothes on. People feel naked if they don't have slides.

—Vern Kelley

Presenters seem to think we are just PowerPoint receptor machines.

—Felicia Marcus

It's not 'show and tell.' Just answer the questions without putting up another chart. Just look me in the eye, and say, 'John, the answer is 6.'

—John Kispert

Depending too much on visual aids, or worse, reading them, can be career limiting in front of senior leadership. Slides are your backup. They're tools to bolster your argument. They cannot be your argument. Ironically, Steve Ballmer, the CEO of Microsoft, the company that makes PowerPoint, famously advised a presenter, "Please, don't show me the deck."

If you are a senior leader in a Fortune 500 company, you have seen perhaps 100,000 slides shown by hundreds of presenters over the years. John Kispert said, "There are weeks when I sit through over 100 presentations." Just imagine how mind-numbing that would be if every one of those presenters comes armed with, say, 10 to 20 slides.

The executives we interviewed were universal in their dislike of slide shows from subordinates. Ned Barnholt commented that he simply could not trust a presenter's depth of understanding if he or she could not speak without slides. Dan Eilers said, "The most powerful slide is no slide, because slides numb the mind."

What these executives want is a discussion, not a slideshow. Following the "10/30 Rule," if you prepare for just 10 minutes of content and figure three minutes per slide, you will need only three slides for a 30-minute presentation. Do have backup slides, though, in case they want to drill down.

Anna Eshoo commented emphatically, "I don't have time for a PowerPoint presentation!" She went on to describe a visual aid fiasco when General David Petraeus buried a congressional delegation with PowerPoint slides in order to avoid confronting the issues they came to talk about:

> The main purpose of our visit was to learn when we could bring the troops home. He said 'Hello.' We sat down in his office, and he immediately began with a PowerPoint presentation. And it went on and on and on.
>
> I had two takes on that PowerPoint presentation: (a) this was an insult to this Congressional delegation, who came here to talk about very specific, serious, profound questions, and (b) that he was playing Beat the Clock, thinking "I'm going to use up all of the time with a PowerPoint presentation, and then look at the clock and say, 'You know what, I'm sorry. I've got to go and meet with the troops now. Nice to see you. God bless you and God bless America,' and hightail it out of there."

General David Petraeus

> He had to be stopped by the leader of the delegation who said: 'General, we appreciate this, but we've traveled halfway across the world to meet with you, to get the answers to the following questions . . .' Petraeus didn't like that. He's accustomed to doing exactly what he wants to do.
>
> If someone thinks that they're going to dazzle a top leader simply with a PowerPoint presentation, they're mistaken. It can be deadly.

A Visual Aid Horror Story

Brenda Rhodes recalled the dangers of over-reliance on the computer and PowerPoint slides:

> I was part of a three-person panel. The computer crashed during the presentation of the speaker before me, and he died with it. He had his entire outline on his PowerPoint, and couldn't do his presentation without the computer. The audience watched him literally sweat—the beads of sweat dropping on the computer—as he tried to get it to work and couldn't. He threw out some summaries and that was the end of it.

Brenda was able to do her presentation without the PowerPoint. She advises, "Don't ever put yourself in a position where you can't just stand and present without visual aids. Know your presentation well enough to do that."

But, in the event you do have to use PowerPoint, here are some quick tips for your slide presentation, not just for executives, but for any audience.

Slide Content and Delivery

Research from Richard Mayer[2] at the University of California, Santa Barbara, Michael Alley[3] at Penn State, and Edward Tufte[4], former Yale professor of statistics, proves that word slides are the least effective way to get your message across. All of these researchers argue for more graphical content on slides: color charts, photos, diagrams . . . whatever would support your message nonverbally.

Tips For Slide Delivery:

- Stand next to the screen, not at the computer. This says, "I'm fully engaged in what I'm presenting."

- Use a remote mouse to advance your slides. This gives you freedom to move around the room and not be tied to your computer.

- Use a mechanical pointer. Laser pointers are popular because they seem cool. Actually most audiences don't like them. In an informal survey, we asked a presenter to do the same presentation in three different ways: pointing to the screen with his hand,

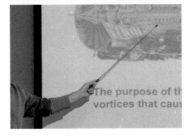

pointing with a mechanical pointer, and pointing with a laser. Of the 50 people in the audience, all 50 preferred the mechanical pointer. Several were adamant that they hated the laser pointer.

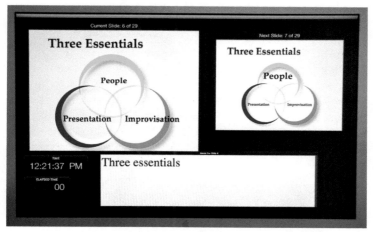

Computer Dual Screen and Notes Function

- Use the dual screen/notes function on your computer. Today's visual aid software in both the Mac and the Windows environments allows you to control your image flow as never before. Your audience will see only the slide you want them to see, while you can see the next slide coming. Also, with the notes section at the bottom of the page, you can simply glance down and get an idea or statistic quickly without fumbling through notes.

- Use the 'B' key. In slide show mode in both Keynote and PowerPoint, the 'B' key on your computer keyboard makes the screen go blank. Press it once to blank the screen, press it again to bring back the image.

There are three benefits to doing this:

1. It creates a "pattern disruption" event which refreshes the brains of your audience members.

2. It draws their attention back to you.

3. It says to the audience, "This conversation is between us; it is not about reading slides."

If you act on nothing else I've recommended in this chapter, do this. Using the 'B' key marks you as a pro.

Whether using word slides or graphics, keep the content big and bold. Your busy, multitasking audiences have zero interest in working hard to decipher what's in your slides. As reported in Fortune Magazine,[5] venture capitalist Vinod Khosla has what he calls the "Five Second Rule." Khosla shows a slide for five seconds, turns it off and asks the viewer what it was about. If the viewer can't recall, the slide is a failure.

Corinne Nevinny

Finally, send slides in advance. This is not only an important part of the preparation; it can also be strategic. As Corinne Nevinny observed, "Send your slides out before the meeting. It prevents the meeting from being a 'free-for-all.' Most people won't read what you send them, and if they feel unprepared, they are less likely to attack your idea."

Summary

If you speak infrequently, chances are you don't think much about your delivery. Most people who take our training programs are unaware of how they look when they present. Usually their delivery hurts their content because they look nervous, which, as we've seen, creates doubt in the audience's mind regarding their mastery of the topic. The good news is that style is easy to master. Nervous, fidgety delivery can easily be fixed by taking a video-based training program and/or getting private coaching. In the meantime remember:

- Look 'em directly in the eyes.
- Use long pauses and lots of vocal variety.
- Use descriptive gestures that are up and out, away from your body.
- To own your space, move with purpose at transitions in your presentation, then plant your feet.
- Keep visual aids to a minimum, but when you do use them, stand next to the screen and point to what you are talking about with a mechanical pointer. (Avoid the laser.) Use the 'B' key to shift focus and to increase your interaction with the audience.

www.powerspeaking.com/chapter13

CHAPTER

14

I Really Did
Give A Damn!

In Part II, you met our six mid-level executives: Todd Lutwak, Julie Patel, Brent Bloom, Sharon Black, Randi Feigin, and Andy Billings. You saw them come face-to-face with the Seven Deadly Challenges. You read the stories of how they got advice from senior executives, learned how to manage the challenges, and then succeeded in their presentations. Mastering the *Speaking Up*® strategies has made a difference in their lives and in the lives of people they work with. After their executive presentations, I sat down and interviewed each of them on video about the key skills they took away from the *Speaking Up*® training and how it has affected their careers and leadership skills.

Todd Lutwak

Speaking Up® is to presentations what the Boy Scout motto is to life—Be Prepared. Too often speakers walk into a meeting with an agenda of what they want or need, not taking full account that there are other people (often more senior) that have a different agenda, timeframe, or expectations. A well-prepared presenter will have a greater understanding of this, and instead of having one approach will be prepared to present their material in a variety of ways. The question should never be, "Did I do a great presentation?" The question should be, "Did I get my point across and did I achieve my intended outcome?"

For example, in my own presentations to senior executives, I prepare myself for different time scenarios. First I learn the material assuming I have the fully allotted time, then I attempt to do it in half the time, and then a third of the time. As a manager this is a good skill to teach your employees. The next time you have a meeting where someone in your group is presenting to you, cut their time in half and leave the remainder for questions and deeper discussion, and see what happens.

At work, I would like to be remembered first and foremost as being a great manager and mentor. I view the success of my work as being the success of the people who work on my teams. Did they have fulfilling and energetic careers that they are proud of?

At home, I would hope my family looks at my work and understands the pride that I take in it. I want my kids to be serious about work and understand that work is something that you should pour your heart into. I want them to know that you should be passionate about what you do. But at the same time, have a good work-life balance. I would never want my kids to think that it was all work, and that I wasn't able to disconnect from work and enjoy the time that we have at home as a family as well.

Julie Patel

I'd like people to know that I really did give a damn about all this stuff. It wasn't just to get a paycheck or to push forward the party line or the company approach. There isn't always a black-and-white answer to everything. You have to balance all the needs of the different people that are involved in an HR situation. I want people to know that I really did care that we got the right outcome, and that is why my presentation was so important.

Connecting with people and participating in direct, honest conversation is important to me. *Speaking Up®* skills have helped create a connection between my values and intentions, and by extension, the people who I work with on a daily basis. It has helped me to find my own voice, which, in turn, serves as a model for others. That is a legacy I want to leave.

Brent Bloom

Speaking Up® has changed the way I go about planning for executive-level presentations. As a result, the amount of time I spend outlining and developing my presentations has been reduced by as much as 75%. Also, the clarity and focus of my message is so much more effective; I get to quicker agreements and have deeper discussions with the executives than ever before.

On a personal level, the application of the *Speaking Up*® methodology has increased my confidence which directly influences others' perceptions of my "executive presence," and that is a key to advancement! I know this training works because people at my presentations, including VP level executives, often come up and ask if I will help them with their next presentation.

In terms of legacy, what I want to be remembered for is that it was both fun and productive working with me. I hope people feel they learned a lot about what was going on and that they had a significant impact on the company and what we were trying to achieve.

Randi Feigin

For my legacy, I want to be known as a person who is passionate and authentic, not just as a manager or an employee, but as a wife, a mother, a sister, a daughter, and a friend. Communication is critical in every relationship and more often it's not what you say that affects people, it's how you say it, both verbally and nonverbally. This came across in a very powerful way during the *Speaking Up*® project. In my second presentation, I was more proactive by working with my sponsor in advance, and I was more assertive in the way I handled the executive interactions. I see examples of this every day in both my professional and personal life.

It is a continuous learning process to seek and understand what type of communication works with which audiences.

What is effective with one group may not work with another. It's a balancing act between the heart and the mind both at work and at home.

Andy Billings

The *Speaking Up*® skills have made me a more effective presenter at the executive level. Specifically, I keep four things in mind:

- First line, bottom line. I get to the point fast. I find this leaves time for discussion and ideas to come from the execs. When execs are talking, they are "selling" to themselves. When I am talking, I am not getting deeper insights into what the decision makers are thinking.

- Be concise. I generate lots of ideas—but too many points detract from my impact. I find things go better when I concentrate on the 20% of my points that will create 80% of the motivation for an executive to say, "Yes."

- It's their meeting—not mine. When I come prepared to support their conversation—and not be so concerned with my own ego—I find we get the best outcomes. And often this is a better solution than I brought to the meeting.

- Be brave enough to be explicit in your "asks." When I am clear in my requests for resources, I am more likely to get a "yes." Everyone thinks they could use more resources. I remind myself to ask for only what I need—but then don't settle for less.

I hope people will remember me as the person who amplified their ideas and helped to support and implement them in a way that otherwise might never have happened.

Sharon Black

Applying the *Speaking Up*® concepts has made a huge difference in my career and in the careers of people who work with me. I am more confident and more comfortable in my own senior executive presentations. In addition, I've been able to pass the skills on to my subordinates. For example, recently my team of five regional managers needed to present to the executive team. As I prepared them for the meeting, we focused on three things:

1. The bottom line statement for each presentation;
2. Using the detail as back up only as needed;
3. A dry run practice session in which I played the senior executives and took them off course and told them to be ready to improvise and make changes on the fly.

The meeting went very fast. Afterwards, my boss gave me a high five. He told the other executive presenters, "Follow Sharon's lead." My team was so surprised that what the executives wanted was the bottom line, not all the detail. Without the *Speaking Up*® training, I wouldn't have done this level of preparation, and my team would have presented way too much detail. When it was over, they were ecstatic.

For my legacy, on a more personal level, I would love for my father to say on a keynote birthday that he is so proud of his daughter and what a difference she made in the community. I think that would be . . . huge. *

---

* At her 50th birthday party, Sharon's father got up and said exactly that. She was included in *The San Francisco Business Times*' "The Bay Area's 100 Most Influential Business Women of 2011."

Summary

Our six heroes took time to reflect on how the *Speaking Up*® training influenced their careers and their leadership. As frequent speakers at the top levels of their companies, the *Speaking Up*® skills have made them more effective executives and better leaders. They also reflected on what they hoped their legacies would be. Similar to what the executives talk about in Chapter 18, they wanted to positively affect their families, their employees, and their companies.

Part III Summary

You can be well-prepared, well-researched, and well-rehearsed, yet your top-level presentation can still career off the track. When that happens, remember:

- Get out of "presentation mode" and into "process mode."
- Be a facilitator. It may account for 80 percent of your success.
- Practice "Deep Listening." This allows you to more fully understand the issues and assures the executives you are someone they can trust.
- Be flexible and improvisational. This can help you guide the meeting to the solution you want.
- Also remember that your presentation skills are not the main event at the top level, your content is. Nevertheless, if you are not a confident speaker, get some video-based training. Don't make your executive audience endure your tentative, uncertain delivery style. It will make it harder for them to retain the value of your message.

Career and Personal Advice from the Top

O ne topic has dominated the world of fad-laden business publications and training for the past 25 years: "Leadership." Like Hollywood sequels, leadership is a topic that seems to be a box office hit year after year. From Tom Peters *(In Search of Excellence)*, to Ken Blanchard *(The One Minute Manager)*, to Jim Collins *(Good to Great)*, to Jim Kouzes and Barry Posner *(The Leadership Challenge)*, there is a seemingly insatiable appetite for research data, Harvard studies, even parables (Spencer Johnson's *Who Moved My Cheese*) about how to lead. Perhaps this is because each year a new crop of MBAs charges onto the playing fields of business with one burning question, "What the hell do I do now?"

While *Speaking Up®: Surviving Executive Presentations* might be considered a business "self-help" book, it is not about how to become a CEO. Neither is it a book about leadership "best practices." This book is directed at those who must speak to top leadership. It offers strategies that will help you get in and out of those presentation rooms successfully. In Part IV, we take a deeper look at who these C-levels are, their lives, their struggles, their worries, their goals, the legacies they want to leave, and most importantly, how they see their relationships with subordinates, especially during presentations.

Why should you care? Why should this matter to you? There are at least two reasons:

1. The more you know about the people sitting around that table, the better your chance of being successful. As I recount what these executives told me about their lives, think in terms of your own top-level executives. What can you learn about them? Where can you find that information? How can you weave that information into your presentations?

2. Whether you ultimately accede to the C-level or any other senior leadership position, your personal life and your business life have an amazing trajectory through the years. You will face many of the same things they have dealt with: successes and failures, mentors, hopes and dreams, and legacies. In their stories you'll see your story.

Audrey MacLean puts it strategically:

> Most executives are trying to "pattern recognize" what you're presenting in the context of their experience in other business opportunities over the years. They're trying to draw this pattern, 'Here's what he's telling me, and it reminds me of this . . .' So the more you know about what their experiences have been, what they've worked on, decisions they've made in the past, the better able you'll be to figure out how they're thinking about what you're telling them.

A body of research supporting Audrey's observation shows that people prefer to do business with people who are like themselves, including beliefs, hometowns, and alma maters.[1]

You have a better chance of building a bridge with executives if you understand something about their personal and business backgrounds. Remember, they are consciously or unconsciously looking for a recognizable pattern in what you are presenting.

For example, if you were presenting to Steve Blank, and you had read his book, *Four Steps to the Epiphany*, you would know how much he values facts about customers based on research via in-person meetings. Getting ready for your presentation, then, you would include fact-based customer information. In your presentation, you might mention how you did

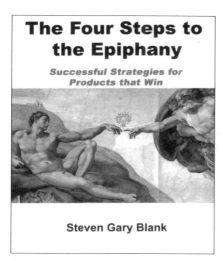

The Four Steps to the Epiphany

Successful Strategies for Products that Win

Steven Gary Blank

Four Steps to the Epiphany

the research and what it means. Steve might pay more attention to your presentation knowing that you share his commitment to customer information.

Here's another example. Let's say you are presenting to Ned Barnholt. On the Internet you can find lots of references to how exposure to Bill Hewlett and Dave Packard shaped Ned's management style at Agilent. If your presentation related in some way to management philosophy, and you mentioned how you were influenced early in your career by a strong mentor, Ned might have a moment of "pattern recognition," and that would help build the rapport that is so critical in these meetings.

Obviously, it is unlikely these particular executives will be in your audience, but think about what commonalities you have with the executives who *will* be in your audience. If there is a link, you and your proposal will receive a warmer reception.

In summary, doing deep homework about the people around the table will reveal ways you can connect with them. Knowing what it is like to ascend to the lofty heights of top-level executive positions not only gives you needed empathy for the people sitting before you, but also gives you clarity about what that path is like. Is it the path you are on? Is this the path you want to be on?

In the concluding chapters of this book, we'll explore three areas of importance to people at the top: parents and mentors, career challenges and advice, and legacy. If your goal is to make it to any senior-leadership position, you will find guidance in the stories of those who've gone before you. Are you ready to shoulder the responsibility? How does it affect family life? What about mentors and support systems? Additionally, knowledge of their struggles will help you understand what they're trying to do.

To get this information, I conducted in-depth interviews with eleven C-level executives about their personal lives and careers: their parents; where they grew up and went to school; the pivotal events in their lives; their mentors; their struggles and self-doubts; lessons learned; even how they want to be remembered by their children. As you read their stories, advice, and counsel, reflect on your own business and personal life. What can you take away from their experience to help you carve out your own future?

15

Parents, Mentors, and Role Models

Looking Over the Pickle Barrel

Who's the teacher? Who's the student?
—Leo McCarthy
Former California Lieutenant Governor

We're all just links in a chain.
—Bob Dylan

Think back to your formative years: grammar school, high school, even college, and your first job. Who was there for you? Who saw the talent, the intelligence, the possibilities in you that you could not see in yourself? Does more than one person come to mind? An uncle or an aunt? A grandparent, a neighbor, or a teacher?

For Steve Blank, who grew up in New York City, the seeds that would lead to his achievements were sown by his immigrant parents:

They came over in steerage, and took the tour of New York Harbor under the Statue of Liberty. They came through Ellis Island and worked in sweatshops in the Lower East Side of New York. They dreamed of opening a grocery store. After working in the garment district for a decade, they wanted to work for themselves.

I guess you could say my parents did a start-up and were small

145

business entrepreneurs. Rather than taking over the universe, they simply wanted to feed the family. They owned a little grocery store and their entire team was my two parents, and then my sister and me when we were old enough and could see over the pickle barrel. Then it was our turn.

The executives talked about two huge influences in their early lives and in their successes: their parents and their mentors. They started life with bonds to their parents and families, then later met people who helped shape their futures. They learned ways of being from both sources that powered them to top positions in corporate America.

Audrey MacLean credits much of her success to growing up in the Darwinian environment of a large family. "In a family of ten, you turn your head and your brother steals the meat off your plate. And if you don't say something interesting at the table, the conversation jumps quickly to someone else."

How these early influences shaped their destinies was a major theme in the interviews.

The executives shared their parent and mentor stories, often through tears of gratitude. Taken together, their stories show us why finding and using your champion is so critical, and how such influence can last your entire lifetime.

As you read the following stories from our senior executives, think about who those mentors have been for you. Are they still alive? Have you seen them lately? Have you told them how their influence has affected you?

Seeing Potential
& Changing Lives

Steve Blank advised, "If you're lucky in your twenties and thirties, you will find somebody who will take an interest in your career, and will change your life." That mentor's impact often starts when he or she sees abilities and potential in you that you can't see in yourself.

That's what happened to Anna Eshoo. When she talks about Leo McCarthy, California Lieutenant Governor from 1983 to 1995, her voice gets quiet. "He took me under his wing. I didn't see in myself what he saw in me." Anna recalled their deep friendship and his encouragement of her political career:

Anna Eshoo

Leo McCarthy

He came to a speaking event early in my first run for Congress. After it was over, I called him at home since I didn't get a chance to talk to him afterwards. I said, 'How did I do?' He said simply, 'Who's the teacher? Who's the student?'

Anna was very close to her parents who attended her swearing in as a member of Congress in 1993. She recalled, "Every time I go on the Floor (of the House of Representatives) I look up to the section where they sat in the gallery that day in 1993. I sense them being there and watching everything that I do."

Felicia Marcus

Felicia Marcus grew up in Los Angeles and started her career as an attorney with an emphasis on environmental law. She later went to work for the City of Los Angeles and was soon appointed by Mayor Tom Bradley to run the Board of Public Works. When offered the position by the deputy mayor, Felicia thought he was crazy. "How can I possibly run this giant department?" she asked him. "I don't know how to manage." He said, "I've been watching you and how you're working with the engineers and everyone on the other side of this lawsuit.

You're doing exactly what a good manager does to help people see it a new way."

She took the job. "Suddenly I was running the largest public works department in the country when I was in my mid-thirties. I see now I am a much better manager than I ever would have been a lawyer," she told me.

> The mentor/teacher is the person who sees who you are, sees your beauty, falls in love with it, helps and inspires it, giving it a chance to bloom in the world.
>
> —James Hillman[1]
> Jungian Analyst

The Big Picture

Felicia and Anna didn't see in themselves the abilities that others saw in them. Similarly, mentors can provide critical perspective that can shape your future.

Dan Eilers grew up in Portland, Oregon, the only child of a truck driver father and a homemaker mother. During his extremely modest start in life, he watched TV programs like "Leave It to Beaver," and saw an upper-middle class way of life that he hoped to achieve some day. His family physician, Dr. Joseph Trainer, saw potential in Dan and encouraged him to go to college, and then on to business

Dan Eilers

school at Stanford. Only after a rewarding career in Silicon Valley as a CEO of several companies and now as a venture capitalist, did Dan return to his native Oregon.

Dan said his father never understood his corporate life. Dan recalled:

> He would say, 'You should have gone to work at 8 and left at 5. Why did you work 70-hour weeks? You went to college. That should have meant you'd work only 40-hour weeks. You lost yourself for all those [corporate] years, but now you have reclaimed what I brought to you.'

Dr. Trainer saw the bigger world that lay ahead for Dan, though his father could not. However, his father would have appreciated that his son is now able to return to his roots—hunting, fishing, and hiking where they used to go as father and son so many years ago. And that, too, is part of the mentoring that has molded Dan's life.

Beacons

Mentors can also help show you the way once you've identified your path. "When I was six years old I knew I wanted to be a CEO and an electrical engineer," Rick Wallace told me. "I didn't know what either of those things were, but that is what my grandfather was."

Rick Wallace

Both of Rick's parents were college professors. His grandfather, David Sciaky, founded and ran Sciaky Brothers which was an innovator and global leader in welding technology. Rick remembers one of the highlights of his childhood as watching the Apollo moon landing in which Sciaky Brothers had been responsible for developing the welding technology that was deployed in the program. David Sciaky received the French Legion of Honor medal in recognition of his contributions to science and technology. His grandfather's success and accomplishments made quite an impression on Rick:

> To me it was about what technology could do, what it meant to own a company, and to run a company. I didn't know what all that meant, but I had this idea from being a little boy around my grandfather's company.

Years later, Rick was offered a sales position. Not sure what to do, he consulted with his grandfather, then in his late eighties, who said, "Look, you could do that. You'd get a nice car. You'd probably get a good salary. You could make good money. But you'll never go back to being an engineer. So you'll just have to decide if that's what you want to do." Rick declined the sales job.

Dan Warmenhoven recalls having many mentors along the way, but none greater than his father, Pete Warmenhoven, and his boss at IBM, Frank Metz:

Dan Warmenhoven

> My father worked in fresh produce packaging. The plant had about 300 warehouse people. Every morning he would walk the line, and everybody knew him, and they knew him as Pete, not as Mr. Warmenhoven. He knew most of them by name. That said something to me about how you interact with a team. It wasn't leadership through power; it was leadership through personal connection. That had a huge influence on me.

Later in his career when Dan worked for Frank Metz, the CFO of IBM, he learned a critical lesson about modesty. Dan watched as Metz made recommendations about a controversial issue facing the company. After the meeting, Dan said:

> 'Frank, that was just brilliant how you resolved that issue,' to which Metz responded, 'Don't get too enamored with it. That decision will stick on the wall for about 24 hours. Those guys know I don't have the final authority to make that decision.'

Dan observed:

> He was very matter of fact about it. He understood his role, and he understood the limits of his power. He knew there'd be an escalation from the side that lost. To him it wasn't an affront in any way, and he also didn't feel as though the issue was over. It was a very philosophical kind of response. It said to me, 'Don't get too carried away with your power, because the dynamics of people and organizations often are more powerful than any position power that may be entrusted to one person.'

For Dan, the stories of these two mentors seem to say, "Don't get a big head just because you're the boss."

Tricks of the Trade

Mentors teach you the tricks of the trade. At age 43, Brenda Rhodes was running a $10 million business that was going under because it was running out of cash. "I didn't know how to read a financial statement or a balance sheet," said the CEO who was raised on a sugar beet farm in Washington. "I didn't know the language of finance. I was faking it."

Determined not to allow her lack of knowledge about finance to hold her back, she enrolled in a three-year Harvard Business School executive program, called OPM: Owner, President, Manager. Her finance professor, Samuel Hayes, told her, "Brenda, you are brilliant operationally. I can tell. If you'll stay with me through the basics, you'll have that magical combination. I can teach anybody finance, but I can't teach everybody operations. They just don't have that same feel for the people and the process that you have."

Brenda recalled:

> Samuel Hayes gave me the confidence that I could actually learn finance, and so I did. The first year they taught me all about how to read a balance sheet, how to make a profit and loss statement work, what the levers were, and how to make the changes in my business to be successful.

Brenda Rhodes

As Brenda went through the program, she built her business from $10 million to $28 million, to $40 million. Now she could negotiate with the bank because of her new finance skills. She then learned about venture capital and public markets. By the final year of the program, Brenda had taken her company public and raised $80 million.

She credits Samuel Hayes with teaching her what she needed to know. Mentors will teach you the tricks of the trade.

Hard Lessons

In his late 20s, Steve Blank was flying high as a VP of Marketing in a high-tech startup. During a high-level specifications meeting with engineers and scientists jumping into the discussion, he felt the need to give his opinion. After about five minutes, Allen Michels, the CEO, said, "Are you through?"

Instead of recognizing that things weren't exactly going well, Steve's ego drove him to continue for another few minutes. "I thought I was a genius," he recalled. When he was done, Michels just looked at him. "Now are you done?" he asked as the people in the room who knew him began backing up their chairs, fully aware of what was about to hit.

Steve Blank

Then Michels got in real close to Steve's face, like a Marine drill sergeant, and started screaming at him:

> You're an embarrassment to the profession of marketing. You don't know a damn thing of what you're talking about. This room is full of people who've had 20 years of experience in talking to customers and understanding their needs. You don't have a clue about what these customers need, and therefore you're just wasting our time. Get the hell out of the building. Get the hell out of my company . . . and take the damn VP of Sales with you. Don't come back until you know who our customers are.

Steve recalled, "I'd been fired publicly, and humiliated."

Allen Michels became a mentor for Steve because he'd taught him a critical lesson: that facts about customers, rather than opinion, are what matter. That message not only changed Steve's life, but his entire career. Although delivered by a two-by-four, the message is something Steve employed in growing his future businesses and now teaches to hundreds of students in his MBA classes at Berkeley and Stanford. He calls it

Customer Development. He advised, "When marketers open their mouths, no one wants to hear their opinions. What they ought to be talking about are facts from customers."

A second hard lesson. Not only did Steve Blank learn about the importance of knowing your customers from being fired by Allen Michels, he learned about consultative selling from one of the masters, Rob VanNaarden. As a young salesperson who was, in his own words, "not only completely clueless but enormously arrogant," he found out the hard way that his approach wasn't working. During one critical sales call, Steve had tried to make the sale by telling the engineering staff how smart he was and what idiots they were for not buying the products he was offering sooner. To his chagrin, he and Rob, his VP of Sales, were escorted out of the building.

A while later, Steve went on another sales call with VanNaarden who said:

"This time, let me handle it." Steve watched in amazement as Rob opened with trivia about the local high school sports scores, and talked about family and kids. Steve was thinking, "What is all this wasted time about? Let's get to the technology." Rob went on to compliment the prospect. "Listen, I'm almost embarrassed we're here. You guys are the smartest engineers the industry has ever seen. If you had the money we raised, and if your bosses had been smart enough to give it to you, you could have built better computers than we ever have."

Steve could not believe how much time was being wasted. Finally, the prospect said to Rob, "Well listen Rob, now that you understand all that, we're ready to talk. What do you have to show us?"

Steve continued to work with Rob who taught him about emotional intelligence and the art of consultative selling. It changed his business career forever.

Criticism as a "Present"

In addition to Rick Wallace's grandfather, another early influence in his career was his boss, Gary Dickerson. Gary called Rick into his office one day and said, "I have a present for you." Gary proceeded to give him some harsh criticism. Rick said, "How is this a present?" Gary responded, "No one else will tell you, and it will help make you more effective in your job." Today, Rick does not hesitate to give difficult feedback to people, still using the idea that it's a gift.

Role Models to Emulate

Ned Barnholt

Role models practice the kind of leadership you want to strive for. Ned Barnholt had just joined Hewlett-Packard Labs when he was asked to fix Bill Hewlett's stereo, which he did. When Bill came to pick it up, he engaged Ned in a personal conversation about his career and about the company.

It was a life-changing moment for Ned. "Bill just chatted and asked 'Why did you join the company? How do you like it here? What attracted you to HP?' He spent 20 minutes talking to me as this young engineer, right out of school."

Ned added:

Bill Hewlett

> That always impressed me. The CEO of the company cared about individuals at the entry level. When I became CEO I remembered that story and what a big difference it makes if I can take time to go around the labs or different places in the company to shake hands, talk to people, and get to know them a little personally. 'Why did you join? How's it going?' That became a key part of my management style and philosophy.

Ned also recalled sitting next to Dave Packard at a dinner event and how genuine, open, and approachable Dave was.

Those early encounters with Bill Hewlett and Dave Packard had an impact on Ned's management style for the rest of his life. He remembered what Dave Packard used to say, "You need to be hard-headed and soft-hearted." Throughout his own career as a CEO, Ned made conscious efforts to treat employees as he'd been treated by Bill and Dave.

John Kispert learned a lot about business from his first boss, Billy Helmer, who owed a deli on Long Island where John worked as a 12-year-old. Billy would pick him up at 5:00 AM and drive him to work. Sometimes Billy would take John to the bar across the street about 7:00 AM. "Hey Johnny, watch this," he'd say. Then he would yell out to the entire bar, "Hey, drinks are on me!" and buy a round for everyone. "What do you think every one of those guys is going to do now?" he asked every time before answering his own question. "They'll come walking across the street to the deli to get a hero sandwich or a meatloaf to go with their beer."

But it wasn't just Billy's marketing ploy that stuck with John, it was the dedication to one's business and to one's customers that he learned from his boss. John recalled:

John Kispert

> He was very hard on me. He ran a good shop that did very well. His credo was, 'There's not a moment that you shouldn't be doing something. You're forever trying to take care of people and keep the cycle time of the store moving very quickly.' He impressed that on me, over and over again. There's always a window to be cleaned or a roast beef to be trimmed, or a potato salad to be made, or fresh coffee to be made, or a supplier to be paid. It's a 24-by-7 business and you just stay on top of it. He was constantly on the move. Billy's philosophy applies to any business. I've made it part of my muscle memory, and I carry it with me today.

Support System

A mentor stands solidly behind you, and gives you opportunities you might not otherwise have.

With a degree in agricultural economics, Ginger Graham's first job was with a food production company called Elanco, a subsidiary of Eli Lilly. Ginger, who was born in a rural Arkansas town which she describes as "Five thousand people on a dirt road in the middle of nowhere," recalled, "I had no exposure to row crops, soybeans, cotton, or rice. I was inexperienced in every sense, and I was also the first woman that was hired in that area."

Ginger worked for a district sales manager, Charles Moody, who, along with his wife Anita, became like a second set of parents to the young person away from home. She recalled his support for her:

> He embraced my development and spent a lot of time with me. He helped me understand how to compete, how to learn, how to grow up. I was 21 years old, and he was there when I didn't know I needed someone . . . but did. He gave me great advice and counsel.

Ginger's first sales assignment was in a large territory that had been chopped up into two smaller ones, and the previous sales rep had been reassigned. One giant customer dominated the territory, and they didn't want to do business with a young, inexperienced female sales rep. So they called Charles Moody demanding to have their old sales rep back. He responded, "Gee, it's a shame you won't be doing business with us anymore, but when you're ready, please call Ginger." Ginger said:

> He was willing to forego the business to make a point that he was going to stand by his employees and do what was right. And I admire him for that to this day. We still keep in touch. He's very important to me.

Your Role: Give Back

> The mentor is the one who helps you find your own way, but you have to be open. You have to ask questions. You can't pretend to have all the answers. That takes guts, real guts[1]
>
> —Joseph Campbell

These executives' stories spell out the benefits of having a mentor. Getting one, however, depends in part on the realization that the mentor relationship is a two-way street.

A two-way street means that you aren't just a passive recipient of knowledge. Steve Blank points out how critical it is that the mentee has something to give back. If you have nothing to offer, he suggests, then don't ask somebody to be a mentor. Take classes or hire a coach who can help you meet or exceed your goals instead.

For Steve to take on a mentee, he needs to know that he'll learn something in the process, just as his mentors did when they took him on:

> My mentors saw something in me that made them smarter as well. So now when I mentor people, I am picking, not only people who I think are smart, but when the two of us get together, they make my head spin around as well. It's the combination of that relationship over time that makes a mentorship. If you think you are in a place where you have something to offer, that's different. Then you're ready for mentorship.

Between 1974 and 1977 while writing my PhD dissertation, I worked closely with a psychology professor from San Francisco State University named Bob Suczek (1918–2006). He was such an influence on my research and on my personal development as a psychologist that I dedicated my dissertation to him. When the sometimes grueling process was over and I'd completed my PhD, I wrote a letter to Bob thanking him for his loving guidance. He wrote back saying how much he valued the process and how good he thought the dissertation was. But his final sentence brought me to tears. "What you may not have known, Rick, is that I needed you as much as you needed me."

Bob Suczek

Summary

All the executives I interviewed had somebody along the way who gave them the confidence, the inspiration, and the vision to move up. They mentioned relatives, bosses, CEOs, teachers, even a family doctor. Usually these people could see potential and talent in them that they could not see in themselves.

When you present to the top level, remember the people around that table had mentors early in their lives. They have deep feelings about that experience. While they may see you as the "mentee," and you may see yourself that way too, remember it is a two-way street and you are providing them with information they need to make critical decisions. Keep in mind, they need you as much as you need them.

www.powerspeaking.com/chapter15

CHAPTER

16

Career Challenges

*You, more than any other person, are
responsible for the welfare of all. You have
this collection of responsibilities that make
you different than other people.*

—Mark Leslie

*Pressures come when you get to flying
high and it changes your world so dramatically.*

—Brenda Rhodes

*How you handle it when things are going
well doesn't matter. It's when things
aren't going well—that's when it matters
how you handle it.*

—Rick Wallace

*Being CEO is 100 percent of your life.
Eighty percent of it is crap, but the other
20 percent is so much fun it makes it
worth it. It has a life cost.*

—Ginger Graham

Our executives "opened the kimono" when asked what advice they would give to those aspiring to top-level positions. They shared the reality of the ascent to power. They talked about the impact on their families and about the responsibility of running a major corporation. The bottom line of this chapter is: if you have your sights set on a senior leadership position in a Fortune 500 company, pursue it with your eyes wide open.

Reflecting on the challenges of their careers the executives talked a lot about responsibility. While being a CEO can be the greatest job they ever had, they told me it can also be a heavy weight, one you have to be ready to shoulder if you want to be a top executive.

It's a Heavy Load

The rewards are great, and so are the responsibilities. "When you're CEO, it's about other people all the time," said Mark Leslie. He added:

> I'd go to the company picnic, and I'd see this sea of faces. It's humbling. People relying on the company for their livelihood, their mortgages, their kids' college tuition. You feel the weight of that responsibility. It's not something people talk about.

Dan Eilers agreed:

> Recognize that it is a weighty responsibility. The decisions you make and the actions you take are not just for you. They are for the people who are working for you. My employees are affected by decisions I make and how hard I work. As a CEO, your decisions will affect whether they can feed, clothe, and educate their children.

So, how do you become a leader? "There is no handbook," says Harold Fethe. "There's an expectation that if you are working at this level, you already understand these things or you just figure it out. But there's nobody there to hold your hand or make it easy. It's a Darwinian 'survival of the fittest' mentality."

For Ginger Graham, being CEO is about a larger contribution to society, and on the plus side, the joy of giving people a chance to grow into their destinies:

> It's very sobering to be the executive in charge. You cannot avoid the personal accountability that your decisions have: the opportunity to have impact; to lead; to help form a culture; to inspire people to be great. All of that does wonderful things for society.
>
> So, there's no getting away from the weight of the job. And I was always weighing the wonderful things about being a CEO against the junk that I don't like. It's hard, and it

is a burden. For me, though, to be with people and see them
be all they're capable of and deliver great work was always
more powerful than the negatives of the job.

Being CEO can be a double-edged sword. According to Rick
Wallace:

It's a load. It's also an unbelievable opportunity. It's the best
job I've ever had, but there's stuff I can't control. I'd been
CEO for only five months when the stock option investiga-
tion hit. Next came the downturn and the fate of the company was at risk. I've got 5,000 scared employees. We had
to let some good people go, and our future success wasn't
assured by any stretch.

The challenge in the CEO position is that it is natural to
identify with the job, to become the job. That's dangerous
because the job isn't permanent.

Stress and
Personal Change

One day when she was CEO of Advanced Cardiovascular
Systems, Ginger Graham got a disturbing phone call: "There's
a man in the manufacturing plant with a shotgun." The caller
was urgent and tense, "What should we do? Empty the building? Call the sharpshooters?" Ginger reacted with frustration,
thinking to herself, "Oh my God, I didn't sign up for this."

Susan, 42-year-old senior director at a Bay Area biotech
company, found herself changing as she moved up. In one of
our trainings, she had just heard the tough adjectives people
use to describe their top leadership (see Chapter 2). She got
a faraway look in her eye, like she had a new insight about
something very important. After the workshop, she confided,
"Look, I am moving rapidly up the management chain. I am
headed for the C-suite, and I know I'm becoming a real asshole." She went on, "I am more time-pressured than ever. I
don't have patience to listen to people's problems. I have decisions to make, and quickly. This is just where I want to be in my
career, but sometimes it's not a pretty picture."

The good news in that story is that Susan is clear about
where she is going, and what it will take to get there.

The Personal Price

I have talked to many CEOs who have lost their relationships.

—Brenda Rhodes

It's difficult to be the CEO of a company and satisfy the constituencies you have at work, and also pay sufficient attention to the constituencies you have at home.

—Dan Eilers

Working at the C-level is personally demanding. John Kispert observed:

I'm passionate about what I do, and that commitment is probably the biggest driver for me. I'll lock on what we need to get done and be uncompromising and disciplined about it. That takes physical and mental sacrifice, but it's the only way to get there. So you have to find a way to enjoy that.

The job puts strains on families and marriages. John admits he doesn't see his wife as much as he'd like:

We try to take time to be together one night a week when we can. It's not like we go out a whole lot. We just sit somewhere and get caught up. Vacations are often stunted and slowed down because I'm on the phone all the time.

That kind of single focus, to say nothing of the travel, the time demands, and the pull of various constituencies requires management. The executive must be able to make it all work. Dan Warmenhoven commented that, "If you're going to be able to manage a large corporation, you ought to be able to manage your own life first."

For Dan, the family and the job were both priorities; rather than "either/or," it was "both/and." His solution was to bring the family along on business trips, spend a few extra days, and make it a mini family vacation:

I remember when I was at Hewlett-Packard I had to spend a few days in the UK. I got my wife to come and join me and bring the kids, and we toured old England. I mean the point is you can mix these things together if you are committed to both objectives as being very serious.

Dan was quick to add that his wife let him know when adjustments needed to be made:

Now it helps to have a spouse who hits you upside the head when she (or he) thinks you're getting out of balance, and my wife did. She'd say 'It's time to spend more time at home,' but she was also cognizant of busy periods. Not everything is smooth. There are peaks and valleys, and the key is to make sure when you come off a peak in the company you spend whatever free time you've got back with family. I don't think my children felt deprived of a father, and I don't think my wife felt deprived of a husband. We have a very normal life.

Dan Warmenhoven

That balance eludes many. At least two people felt the stress of their jobs contributed to their divorces. For Brenda Rhodes, the huge change in her financial situation after her successful IPO proved too much for the marriage:

I have since talked to people who've experienced a sudden change in their financial situation, like an IPO. It puts weight on everything in your life, including all your personal relationships. It happened to me. Pressures come when you get to flying high and it changes your world dramatically. I've heard about the same thing happening with lottery winners.

The Myth of "Work/Life Balance"

This issue has been famously addressed by Carol Bartz, well known Silicon Valley CEO, when she noted that "work/life balance" is a myth that only leads to counterproductive guilt for working mothers. She warns, "Women put a lot of pressure on themselves. They think, 'I'm going to cook a great breakfast, wash up the dishes before I leave, take the kids to school, call my college roommate on my way in to work, be a CEO all day, volunteer on the way home, do a little exercising, cook a wonderful dinner, help with homework, and have sex.' I don't think so."[1]

Pick the Right Spouse

Every executive I spoke with was aware that the demands of a big career at the top of a major corporation can wreck a marriage. They echoed a common theme: make sure that the person you partner with understands the nature of your career demands and supports your aspirations . . . and that's just the beginning.

Ginger Graham recommends getting the right life partner and getting help on the homefront:

> There's no doubt that there's a tradeoff off of time. You lose control because your employees, your customers, and your constituents have a lot more say over how you spend your time.
>
> The Number One piece of advice I give young women who want to lead organizations is: pick the right partner. Make sure that you marry a man who loves your capabilities and your potential, and is willing to support you. It must be a partnership that includes family care and the running of the household. If there's someone at home who says every time you work late, 'What are you doing there? Why weren't you home early?' that is not pressure that you can sustain at home and have a growing career.
>
> For many women I say, 'Hire a housekeeper and get over it. Build circles of friends who'll help you. If you have children, have carpool buddies who'll always pick up your kids from school if you miss your flight. And remember you're not in it alone. You're not carrying the load by yourself. You have a partner; you

Ginger Graham

> have family; you have friends; you have neighbors; you have business colleagues. Use that network and don't be afraid to ask for help.'

Brenda Rhodes notes that there are a few men who can support their high-achieving wives, but that's rare:

> I've met some up-and-coming young women executives who have husbands at home that are helping raise their children, that are supporting their wives. It takes an extremely

Brenda Rhodes

self-confident and independent and self-assured man to be with a woman who has the kind of aspirations that I had, and that women who succeed at my level have. If you are a woman who wants to get to the big chair, there are trade-offs. Those trade-offs happen in your relationships.

Dan Eilers reflected on this dilemma in terms of advice for his daughter:

I would say to her, 'Megan, if that's what you want to do with your life (become a corporate executive), that's terrific. I support you fully in that. Just make sure that the guy in your life understands, before you get committed, that that's going to be an element of your life, because it's really important to you.' For me, it was a difficult balance. My heart was always at home. My heart was with my wife, and with our daughter, and yet my customers were all over the world.

Megan Eilers

Along the same lines, Scott McNealy, co-founder and former CEO of Sun Microsystems in a keynote address to the Endeavor Entrepreneur Summit, advised people starting out in business:

Start your company before you get encumbered financially and with kids, because you're going to work a bazillion hours. Also, the most important strategic decision you make in your business career—this might surprise you—is who you choose to have babies with. That person is going to be a big part of your life and if you pick the right person it will make you a better leader, a more focused leader, and a leader who can spend more time on your business without feeling bad about leaving your kids home alone. This is very, very important.

Flying Without Radar

When you run a company you have 1,000 mirrors in the faces of your employees looking back at you. You see your weaknesses pretty clearly.

—Ginger Graham

As you become a senior person in an organization suddenly people don't treat you as a person. They treat you as an obstacle, or as a hurdle, or as a potential foe.

—Felicia Marcus

When I became an Admiral a wise mentor told me, 'While you will never be presented with all the truths and facts, you will never have another bad meal!'

—W. W. Copeland, Jr.
Rear Admiral, U.S. Navy (Retired)

Open communication is critical. The status and power of the CEO position can create serious problems:

- Isolation because of people's fear of being direct
- Executives only hearing reflections of their own views
- Bad decision making because the CEO loses touch with business realities

Brenda Rhodes had a deep concern about communication:

I'm always conscious of how hostile or rewarding the presentation environment is to get the kind of communication I want. If it is too hostile, it will shut people down from giving me the truth, and that would mean I'm flying this airplane with no radar. That would be bad news.

As these executives moved up the hierarchy, people started treating them differently. It was hard to get direct, honest feedback. If people brought good news, they were suck-ups. If they brought bad news, they feared being fired. Consequently, senior leaders can get walled off from reality.

Ginger Graham noted:

You get this funny little business card that says 'CEO.' Nobody ever talks to you anymore. What information finally gets to you has been filtered, sifted, canned, and purified.

The job of a CEO is a very unnatural act. People expect you to always be smart, to have the answers, to never have a bad day, or be in a bad mood. And if you are human, all of those things happen, and then people get afraid when you snap at them. If you pop off an inappropriate comment, they think their career is over.

Each of your actions takes on a disproportionate size, and then the question is, can you be so self-disciplined every day, every moment, every meeting, every presentation to be thoughtful, insightful, and to be aware of what's going on with the person presenting to you and still execute your duties as an executive. It's a very high hurdle, and over time, of course, it's impossible. We're just humans, too.

The best approach is to find a way to relate to all of the people you're working with as humans, so that mistakes are allowed, and yet standards are kept high in the organization because we're all in it together.

In my coaching with first time CEOs, I tell them to remember that it's not their job to know everything, and to, in fact, express themselves as a human who is learning, has interest in others, and needs other people around them to be successful. It's important to build an open environment that's honest and that draws out the opportunity for everyone to speak openly and help each other be successful. I'm guaranteeing a failure over time for a CEO who won't get feedback and isn't accessible to other people.

So, as a CEO you actually live in this artificial bubble where no one tells you the truth, either good or bad. How can you grow, how can you be successful, how can you continue to improve your own capabilities and skills if no one will be straight with you? That's the barrier you have to break down.

Harold Fethe said that it is hard being in the fishbowl:

You can never get off stage. You are constantly in the spotlight, and any unguarded moment can actually hurt your organization or your relationship with another employee. It's a kind of tyranny of being on display all the time.

Mark Leslie was very concerned about his impact as CEO on information flow:

It's very important as your organization gets large to be able to stay in touch with reality. The impact of what you say

Mark Leslie

gets multiplied 1,000 times, and that is a great risk because your voice drowns out other voices. You only hear yourself by reflection, so you stop understanding reality and you make bad decisions.

My goal was to make presenters feel at ease, otherwise they will tell you what they think you want to hear. If that happens, the executives lose touch with what is going on in the business.

Staying True to Your Vision

To get the free flow of information he needs, John Kispert feels he must hold back his opinions:

I'm surrounded by a lot of people—boards, customers, investors, bondholders, employees, consultants—all who want it their way. My job comes down to: what's right for this organization as a whole? If I share what I'm thinking, it only influences people in how they're going to present to me. I need to listen to them all, pull it all together, and make the decision.

The CEO's job means: the buck stops here. The hard part is, how do you listen to all that and not compromise the values, the strategy, and the vision of the organization in making that decision? And that means you're going to disappoint a preponderance of those groups. I'm more and more comfortable with that over the last 10 years. It means a lot of contemplating, generally alone, after I've gathered everything I need to know.

Summary

While the view from the top is spectacular, the journey can be hazardous. The communication challenges are huge. You need to keep the channels open at work and at home as you move up in the organization. In addition, there's the reality that decisions these executives make affect the lives and futures of thousands of people. And all of this is on top of the business pressure to keep the company growing and the investors happy. So I asked our executives for their advice for people on that upward journey. Chapter 17 is about what they said.

www.powerspeaking.com/chapter16

CHAPTER

17

Career Advice

It's not about the Porsche.

—Steve Blank

T here is an old axiom that says we learn from our failures. A Harvard Business School study[1] indicates this may not be the case. While the executives certainly had failures and made mistakes along the way, it would be more accurate to say that they learned from their successes and from their mentors, as well as from their failures.

Here they share some hard-won tips that you will find useful in managing your own career growth.

What's Hot and What's Not

The key to success lies in doing what you love. Brenda Rhodes told me:

> I speak a lot to younger people who are trying to find their careers. And the number one question they ask is, 'Where's the big money going to be in the next decade? What's going to be hot?' I answer, 'What do you love? That's what's going to be hot.'
>
> When I was a teenager, my mother used to take me around to the big homes in Saratoga. I'd ask, 'What does that man do to get that house?' She'd say, 'That man made some sort of a disk thing, computer thing.' I'd point to another house and ask, 'What does that person do to get that house?' She'd say, 'He owned shoe stores.' And so it went from house to house. I quickly put it together that maybe I could be successful doing just about anything, if I loved it.

Ned Barnholt would agree that it's more important to do what you love than to do just "what's hot." He reminds people that a career is a forty-year journey, so doing work that you

169

enjoy, the best that you can, in a good organization is critical. Very few of us will become a CEO, or even work at the C-level, so it's important to get satisfaction at whatever level you are working.

Audrey MacLean said:

> It all starts with your own sense of the value of the product and your commitment to bringing it to market. Then it's a matter of spending a lot of time helping your customers be successful using it.

Aim High

For John Kispert career success is all about setting goals:

> Be uncompromising with your goals. Invest in them. Persist. You're going to run into lots of roadblocks. It will be filled with frustration, and that's really the trick to this whole thing—how you handle the frustrations and get to that goal. That's the skill set companies are looking for: being able to solve problems, and get people to do better than they're doing today.
>
> Leadership is about how to get the best out of people and organizations. Develop the skills of communicating and pulling people along, and making your point, and getting people to coalesce around bigger and broader ideas. Drive for change. Don't be afraid of change. Status quo just kills things.

Career Goals

> My ego was measured by my head count.
>
> —Steve Blank

The real secret to success, according to the executives I interviewed, lies in how you define that success. Steve Blank recalled:

> For the first 10 years of my career, I was focused on being my job title. I was a vice president of a public company when I was 29, and I bought a Porsche the day I turned 29. I used to think that what mattered was the next title. I wanted to be a manager. I wanted to be a

director. I wanted to be a VP. It was all about moving up the ladder so my ego could fill the available slot. Those external trappings sure looked good: bigger office, more head count. Man, that was a career goal. I nailed it. It was exciting. Plenty of people do it that way. You step over other people and you elbow your way up using whatever political and cultural acumen you have.

I contend, though, you'll live a much happier life if you do what's authentic and honest, rather than be a title. Because when you get to the top, after scrambling because you wanted to be VP, you might find out it's pretty empty. It affects your relationships: your family, your spouse, and how you deal with other people. Clamoring up the ladder may affect you in ways you might not like a decade or two later.

A Zen-like Moment

All of a sudden Steve had an insight that changed everything:

After focusing on being my titles for the first 10 years, one day, something snapped. Just snapped. Just a clear break. I realized I was measuring my life by the wrong thing. It was a Zen-like moment. I know exactly what made that happen: I had my first child. You know, if you're single, your whole life is focused on you. It is about you. The first part of my career was pretty selfish. I had kids later in life. I watched some of my peers make choices where they still put work first after having children. And I saw the effect that that had on their kids as they grew up.

Steve Blank

I consciously decided: work is important to me, but now there's something that's more important. That was a big idea for me. Getting that work/life balance was something that made my last decades as an entrepreneur and then as a CEO really different than it was for a number of my peers. And it's why I retired at an early age, to be with my family.

Learn Their Names

The CEO of Elanco got on the elevator with Ginger Graham and knew her name. That affected her so deeply, she has made it a point to learn people's names in companies where she has worked ever since:

> I was one of many junior marketing associates, and brand new to the home office. He was in the elevator with me and addressed me by name, and asked about my transition to the home office. It was so impressive to me that he had taken the time to remember who I was, knew a little about me, and reached out to me. I knew then that I would always work very hard to remember people's names.

Similarly, Ned Barnholt and Dan Warmenhoven saw their role models connect with employees in non-hierarchical ways. They both adopted similar approaches in their own leadership styles.

Empathy and Beer

It may be a cliché to say that it's lonely at the top, but most clichés reflect some truth. As John Kispert pointed out, when the job of the C-level executive means doing what's best for the company regardless of the competing agendas of boards, consultants, investors, bondholders, customers or employees, you're guaranteed to disappoint a lot of people a lot of the time.

Maybe that explains Felicia Marcus' observation that once someone gets into a senior-leadership role, he or she is no lon-

Felicia Marcus

ger treated as a person, but as the enemy. She advises people to get beyond that attitude:

> Think about the boss as a full person rather than as a potential torturer or an irrational person who has too much power over you. Figure out how you can be helpful to them. Part of that is not being afraid to ask

them questions about what they're trying to accomplish and how you can best help them achieve their goals.

Felicia feels a critical career skill is being able to understand how complex the top jobs are and actually extend empathy to the senior people who are running the company. (Recall from the work of Krause and Keltner, in Chapter 2, that the subordinate is unlikely to receive much empathy in return.) She recommends finding informal ways to get to know the boss and even invite him or her out for a beer and engage with them where they don't have to be the decision maker. "That is more important to them than you might realize."

Strive to Build a Team

It is a false idea that some individual or superstar CEO uniquely makes great things happen. That is very misleading. There's nothing that can be associated with my career as a success that I did alone.

—Ginger Graham

Heroes are important but they're probably not the best people to manage an organization over time.

—John Kispert

Asked about career success, the executives talked about collaboration and teamwork. Not only was teamwork a hallmark of the C-level executives' own careers, they also expected it in their subordinates.

John Kispert prizes a teamwork attitude in future leaders:

Teamwork and the ability to work "across the aisle" are paramount. You have to be cognizant of that as you are growing people and looking for people to promote and bring up in the organization. Who are the people that have that raw ability to bring out the best in others? Frankly, that's a big challenge that anybody like myself has every day. For the health of an organization, it is probably the number one challenge.

In the course of being CEO of several companies, Dan Eilers learned that he couldn't do it all himself. Success is a team effort:

I learned that no one really works directly for me, but rather that we're all in it together. We're all here to grab customers, pull them in, do right by them, and to give them something unique and better than the competition is giving them. Better, faster, cheaper. And that's our role in life. That's what we're here to do. And to the extent we can all rally around that together, that works far better than an individual focus. It's a huge amount of team building.

From the first days of Dan Warmenhoven's involvement with NetApp, the management team was committed to a collaborative model based on teamwork:

The idea was that people who are feeling part of a team where their voice is heard, where they feel like they have the support of their teammates who are moving in the same direction, would be higher performing and produce a better outcome. And that, in fact, is the way it's worked out.

The ability of people to team together effectively, to get something where the whole is greater than the sum of its parts is absolutely essential. Great teams can do great things. The collaborative scheme was put together here as a core cultural component right from the time I started.

For Ned Barnholt, the individual getting credit is not the point. What matters is how the organization uses the idea:

The important thing is that you had a role in helping move the organization along. Don't get hung up on who gets credit for what. Just do the right thing and do it consistently over and over again, and you'll get recognized and rewarded.

Personal Growth

Reflecting back on her time as a CEO, Ginger Graham, commented that teamwork was not just about a higher performing company, it was also about personal development and about the fun of growing something great. Although Ginger didn't use the words of psychologist Abe Maslow, she seems to be saying that through teamwork people can become "self-actualized" at work:

Great things are accomplished at great expense, personally. People sacrifice. They give up time. They work long hours. They have horrendous travel schedules. They expend per-

sonal energy and take risks. That's how you make things happen that matter. And that always was based on a group of people around me who were willing to bet with me, not against me, or not in spite of me, but with me. Who threw their chips in and said, 'Yes, we're in.'
That is how the fun happened.
That is how work was exciting.
That is how contributions were created.
That is how all of us grew up and were better people for it.

Ginger had additional sage advice for the aspiring senior-level leader:

Realize the more you give away power, the more you share power. The more you include other people in the great successes, the more powerful and the more successful you become. It's by building others up that you become successful. Leaders create leaders, not followers.

Remember to Laugh

Finally, Dan Eilers counseled up-and-comers along with those who have arrived to "keep your cool no matter how intense the pressure and to keep a sense of humor." He recalled how President Ronald Reagan always managed to inject humor into a situation no matter how tense. Looking up from the gurney after being shot, he said to the ER physician, "Well, Doc, I sure hope you're a Republican."

Summary

There you have it—career challenges (Chapter 16) and career advice from those who've struggled up the mountain before you. Even though you may not have your sights set on a C-level position, what they have described here is counsel worth considering at any level:

- Question the notion of "work/life balance"
- Choose the right spouse
- View critical feedback as a gift
- Connect personally with employees
- Have empathy for your bosses and think of them (and treat them) as real people

- It is more about the team than the individual "star"
- Empower others to gain power
- Don't take your role too seriously, there is more power in the organization than in the individual

www.powerspeaking.com/chapter17

Legacy

My father would say, 'She did pretty good, for a girl.'

—Ginger Graham

We forget that as executives we've acquired a hard-fought body of knowledge. When we retire, we go away and it's lost. That's such a waste.

—Steve Blank

The famous psychoanalyst, Erik Erikson (1902–1994), suggested that the middle adult years, ages 40 to 65, are characterized by the need to give back to the next generation:

> The fashionable insistence on dramatizing the dependence of children on adults often blinds us to the dependence of the older generation on the younger one. Mature humans need to be needed. Each adult must have some way to satisfy and support the next generation. A person does best at this time to put aside thoughts of death, and balance its certainty with the only happiness that is lasting: to increase by whatever is yours to give, the goodwill and higher order in your sector of the world.[1]

What the executives told me about the legacies they hoped to leave fits with Erikson's ideas completely.

Family

For some, the family legacy was most important. Dan Eilers said:

> I hope my legacy is in my family. I hope my daughter feels that I've been there for her, that I've supported her, and that she is going to be her personal best in part because of the

values that I brought to her, and because of the coaching that I've done with her along the way, in addition to her own very hard work.

Steve Blank said:

The most important thing is being a great father. On your tombstone would you rather have, 'He never missed a meeting' or 'He was a great dad'? I pick the last one.

Company

Others focused on their professional accomplishments. Dan Warmenhoven said:

Building a great company is the legacy I want. When I came into NetApp, the conventional wisdom was you had your choice between two objectives:

1. You can have a really high-performance organization, but it's probably going to chew people up, and wear them out, or
2. You can have one that has a high degree of concern for individuals, a place people like to work, but performance would be compromised.

I believed we can do both. We can have an extraordinarily high-performance company, and have a place that's also a great place to work. We've beaten Sun, HP, and IBM in market share . . . and we were ranked number one on the Great Places to Work Survey in the United States a couple of years ago. That was a culmination of my personal career goals.

Even though Steve Blank felt that family would be his most important legacy, he also wanted to be known as a teacher and an educator:

I think my teaching at Stanford and Berkeley might be of most lasting importance. I'd also like to be remembered for the work I've done with customer development, and the notion that start-ups are different organizations than large companies.

Ned Barnholt said:

I'd like to be remembered as somebody who left organizations better than they were before. When I was CEO and we were growing the company, I felt very good that I had a hand in helping create jobs for people. People's livelihoods were at stake, and that's a lot of responsibility and stress, but I also felt satisfaction because we created an environment where people realized their own career growth and were successful.

Most important for me is how people feel I am as a person. Am I trusted? Am I respected? I'm not somebody that puts me ahead of the organization. I'm not a big ego guy. I just hope that people would say, 'Ned can be counted on. He delivers. He's a good leader, and he's somebody you can trust, and he's well-respected for what he does.'

Employees

Some focused on their impact on the people who worked for them. Ginger Graham told me:

I'd like to be remembered as someone who invested deeply in the people who worked around me and that everything that was accomplished, was accomplished together, and all of us benefitted from that. We grew personally and professionally, and we were rewarded financially.

Ginger has blazed a leadership trail, especially for women. She was sought out by women in business because she was such an effective role model as a female leader. At a huge company dinner party, one woman who was inspired by Ginger, touched her deeply:

We used to have all company holiday parties every year where employees could bring a family member or significant other. The company put it on to thank the employees for all they had done. I remember one party where a young woman came to my table and crouched down beside me and she had big tears rolling down her face. She said 'I need to talk to you.' I was immediately taken aback thinking, 'Oh, what happened? What's gone wrong?'

There was nothing wrong. She wanted to tell me that she had decided that she was going to quit working and go back to college. She was going to get a degree because she now could see that there were so many opportunities for her that she didn't know about before.

It was a very emotional moment for me. I was so moved by this bright young woman who had the courage to jump, to lose her job, to give up her income, to take a risk, and to go for more education because she knew that there were opportunities in the world to make a difference, because she saw other women role models in the company. Apparently, I was one of those lights for her.

It is just this kind of leadership legacy that Ginger wants to leave, an ambition prompted in large measure by her parents:

> My parents don't value the trappings of life. They value hard work, honesty, giving back, making a contribution, being a good person. And they encouraged me my whole life to do anything and everything I could do. My mom thought I'd be the first female Secretary of Agriculture. So they had big aspirations for me, but it was always to do good while I was doing well. And so if the stock price was down or things weren't going well at work, my parents didn't care. What they wanted to know is: Was I a good person? Was I doing the right thing? Was I giving back? Was I sharing the benefits of my labors with others? And, would I be known as someone that people could count on in the end?

For Felicia Marcus, positively impacting the individuals in her organizations is as important as moving those organizations forward. She said:

> I'd like my legacy to be that I've made a difference in the organizations that I've been a part of, and that they've been seen by the outside world as more effective, dynamic, and results-oriented when I left.
>
> I pride myself on the fact that I have been able to help people so that the light bulb goes on over their heads, realizing that now they can do something they didn't realize they could do.

Summary

Reflecting on their legacies, the executives wanted to have positive effects on the people in their lives both at home and at work. They hoped to leave their companies changed for the better, a bit like Henry David Thoreau who proudly returned his neighbor's ax sharper than when he borrowed it. They wanted their companies to be more productive and better places to work than when they came on the scene. They wanted employees to feel more empowered and be more self-actualized.

www.powerspeaking.com/chapter18

Part IV Summary

As you finished Chapter 18 you might be wondering, "What is all this personal material doing in a business self-help book about strategies and techniques for giving winning presentations to senior leadership?" Good question. Answer: The more you know about the backgrounds, the successes, the failures, and the values of people at the top, the more prepared you'll be when you present to them, or move up in your own career.

In Part IV, the executives talked about their early influences and the people who changed their lives. They described the pleasures and the pain of running large corporations. They also shared advice for those wanting to move up, as well as the legacies they hope to leave behind. These conversations were more personal, deeper, and more insightful than I could have imagined going into the project. I selected passages from the interviews that I felt would be most helpful to you. I hope all of these lessons learned will help make you a more savvy presenter when you enter that senior-level presentation room.

Conclusion

I f this book is about anything, it is about the search for collaboration within an often brutal corporate landscape filled with bright, competitive people driven by the demand for quarterly profits. In Part I, we saw the pressure executives are under and their lack of job security. That impacts your interactions with them, which then drives the triumph or failure of your presentations and perhaps of your career. Given the stew of performance pressure, personality variables, time constraints, and the urgency of getting what you need from them, you need all the success strategies you can muster. That is what Parts II and III were about.

In Part II, our six management heroes entered the presentation room and learned some hard lessons. The first time out they failed miserably. After getting advice from top-level executives, they came back and were successful. They mastered the "Seven Deadly Challenges" of the boardroom. These strategies are easy to learn and easy to use. The trick is to remember what they are. Before your next top-level presentation, go back to Part II and do a quick review.

In Part III, we explored how to develop and deliver a senior-level presentation. The demand of senior leadership to get to the point and be flexible dictates the presentation design. Remember two things: 1) Content is king at the top level, and 2) Poor delivery skills can torpedo a well-constructed presentation. Using the delivery tips in Chapter 13 will keep your audiences engaged, and your content clear. We also explored what Steve Kirsch might call "The 80/20 Rule," which says that your success may be 80 percent determined by your ability to facilitate the discussion and only 20 percent determined by the content.

In Part IV we dug deeper into the life experiences, the values, and the careers of 11 executives. Your career journey may be different from theirs. But even if you have no plans to obtain a seat at the table, knowing what they care about, what has moved them, and what they have learned along the way, will surely give you an advantage.

While presenting to senior people can be intimidating, it can also be full of opportunity. Look at it as a chance to collaborate with the people who run your organization. Dan Warmenhoven put it best:

> There are corporate cultures where they grind people up, but it's very rare. They want you there or they would not put you on the agenda. They're interested in your message, and getting to know you as an individual. They'll be testing you to see how well you understand your topic, but don't panic. Remember they're on your side. We're all part of the same team. They want you to be successful.

As this book is going to press, the world economy is very uncertain. The fate of the Euro and even the European Union is shaky. The stock market is experiencing wild swings daily, and a number of Middle Eastern countries are in chaos. What lies ahead is hard to tell. While there will always be uncertainty in business, and in the economy in general, one thing is clear: people who can get their points across to senior decision makers will be valued by their organizations. The skills you have learned in *Speaking Up®: Surviving Executive Presentations* will help keep your career on track, regardless of the turmoil around you.

Glossary

10/30 Rule   This rule is the ratio of content to discussion. For a 30-minute time slot, prepare just 10 minutes of material. Expect 20 minutes of discussion.

30-Second Rule   With smartphones so prevalent, you have 30 seconds to announce why you are there and what you want. After that, the executives are surfing the net.

Alpha Male (Female)   This term describes a very assertive, controlling person who may dominate meetings by a vocal, emotional, and power differential.

'B' Key   To blank the screen during visual aid presentations using PowerPoint or Keynote, press the 'B' key on your computer keyboard. To see the visual again, press the 'B' key again.

C-Level   An executive whose title starts with a 'C,' e.g., Chief Executive Officer (CEO), Chief Financial Officer (CFO), etc.

Coach   Someone who can help you prepare for *Speaking Up*®. This will be a person who has prior experience with the group you are addressing.

Context   At the beginning of the presentation, explain why this topic matters, the history, and perhaps who else has been involved.

Delivery Style   The mostly nonverbal ways you deliver the message, i.e., gestures, stance, movement, vocal and facial animation, pausing, and eye contact.

Dry Run   A dry run is a rehearsal with colleagues who will give you an audience for a practice session, including tough questions and interruptions.

Dual Screen Mode   Your computer image includes both the current and upcoming slide. The audience sees only the current slide.

Elevator Pitch   A brief summary of your presentation that includes your (P) position, (R) reason, (E) evidence (P) position: PREP. The elevator pitch can be delivered in less than a minute.

Executives   In its most general usage, executives may include anyone from the C-level on down to director level. (The definition varies from one company to another.)

Facilitation (80/20 Rule)   Managing the discussion among meeting participants and lowering resistance through listening, paraphrasing, synthesizing, and providing feedback and direction. According to one CEO, 80% of your success depends on your ability to facilitate the discussion while only 20% depends on content.

First Line, Bottom Line   This is what you want from the meeting. The bottom line could include head count, project approval and budget, executive buy-in, etc. It is critical to state the bottom line at the beginning of the meeting.

Framed Discussion   This term is used to describe an executive presentation.

Graceful Disengagement   If all else fails, stop wasting everyone's time, and acknowledge it is time to stop. Agree to come back later to another meeting.

Hidden Agenda   Issues, perhaps long simmering, can derail the orderly flow of the meeting and sometimes create an executive food fight.

Homework   Significant time must be spent preparing for the meeting, beyond just the content, slides, and rehearsal. Examples: "socializing" the issues to get advanced perspective and buy-in, surfacing arguments and positions, researching who will be in the meeting, sending review materials in advance, etc.

Improvisation (A common term in both jazz and stand-up comedy)   Both jazz musicians and stand-up comics will take what is happening in the moment and move it in a new direction. Similarly, speaking at the top-level requires flexibility to move in and out of content, the emotion in the room, and the needs of the moment.

New Mind Set   *Speaking Up*® requires a shift in approach in many areas: content, timing, Q&A, visual aids, shifting agenda, etc.

Paraphrasing (Active Listening)   Paraphrasing is reflecting back (in your own words) what a questioner is saying or asking. It is the backbone of listening and facilitation skills.

Process Skills   That ability to "read the room," acknowledge what is going on, and move in a new direction.

Question Behind the Question   A simple question may be covering a deeper issue. The presenter's ability to tease out that deeper meaning will help the flow of the meeting.

Read the Room   Reading the room is understanding the individual and group dynamics during the meeting. Being sensitive to body language and other nonverbal cues is critical to being able to use this skill. It is both an internal (notice what is happening and determining a strategy) and an external (addressing the issue and determining the next steps) process.

Remote Mouse   This tool allows you to move through your slides from anywhere in the room without needing to stand at the computer.

Respectful Collaboration   Although *Speaking Up®* can be stressful, the executives will respond positively if you come with an attitude of collaboration rather than one of fear or confrontation.

ROI   "Return on investment," indicates to executives how the company will benefit by doing what you are recommending. ROI is most often a financial risk assessment. For an investment, how much return will there be?

Seating Etiquette   Not directly stated, there are rules about who sits at the executive table. In many top-level meetings, the presenter demonstrates respect by standing at the front of the table, not sitting with the executive team.

Senior-Executive Filter   Filter out raw data and deep detail for the fast-paced executive meeting. Have in-depth, backup information if requested.

Seven Deadly Challenges: These seven challenges are the most common problems that can knock a presenter off track during a top-level meeting.

   Decision Maker Leaves: Without warning, s/he gets up and leaves the room.

   Disengaged Executives: Executives lose interest in the presentation and begin checking email, surfing the net, or side talking.

   Food Fight: Executives are arguing with each other and ignoring the agenda and the speaker.

   Energetic Discussion: Executives are thoroughly engaged, offering new ideas, and building on the presenter's agenda.

   Side Talk: Two or more senior people begin talking among themselves.

   Time Cut: You expected twenty minutes on the agenda and suddenly you have five.

   Topic Change: Executives change focus of the meeting away from the agenda.

Signal-to-Noise Ratio Signal is your message, stated strongly and clearly. Noise is distraction. For example, too much information on your slides or nervous mannerisms get in the way of communication. Senior-leaders want the signal, not the noise.

Speaking Up® Framework The framework is a way to organize and prepare a senior-level presentation that focuses on putting your bottom line up front, supporting that statement mostly with data (not stories), and including a clear ROI statement.

Sponsor Your sponsor is usually in your functional organization and is the person who gets you on the agenda and brings you into the meeting.

Sponsor (Virtual) Your virtual sponsor may be several levels above you—and may be someone you have never met. Nevertheless, s/he has a stake in you being successful.

Type 'A' Personality Many executives have been described as hard-charging, proactive, impatient, and often aggressive personalities. This description overlaps with the "alpha male/female" syndrome.

References

Alley, Michael. *The Craft of Scientific Presentations.* Springer-Verlag, New York, NY, 2003.

Beck, Melinda. "Are Alpha Males Healthy?" *Wall Street Journal,* September 13, 2011.

Blank, Steven. *Four Steps to the Epiphany.* Self published, 2007.

Bryant, Adam. *The Corner Office: Indispensable and Unexpected Lessons from CEOs on How to Lead and Succeed.* Times Books, Henry Holt and Company, LLC, New York, NY, 2011.

Cialdini, Robert B. *Influence: Science and Practice.* Pearson, Boston, MA, 2009.

Ciampa, Dan. "Almost Ready: How Leaders Move Up." *Harvard Business Review,* January, 2005.

Conger, Jay A. *Winning 'Em Over: A New Model for Managing in the Age of Persuasion.* Simon and Schuster, New York, NY, 1998.

Cousineau, Phil. *Once and Future Myths.* Conari Press, Boston, MA, 2001.

Coyne, Kevin and Coyne, Edward. "Surviving Your New CEO." *Harvard Business Review,* May, 2007.

Erikson, Erik. *Childhood and Society.* W. W. Norton, New York, NY, 1963.

Flynn, Francis and Anderson, Cameron. *Too Tough, Too Soon: Familiarity and the Backlash Effect* (working paper, Stanford University).

Davis, Richard. *The Intangibles of Leadership.* Times Books, New York, NY, 2011.

Goldstein, Noah J., Martin, Steve J., and Cialdini, Robert B. *Yes! 50 Scientifically Proven Ways to Be Persuasive.* Free Press, New York, NY, 2008.

Gordon, Thomas. *Leader Effectiveness Training.* The Berkeley Publishing Group, New York, NY, 2001.

GovernanceMetrics International. "CEO Pay Back on the Rise in 2010." June 7, 2010.

Hackman, Richard. "Why Teams Don't Work." *Harvard Business Review,* May, 2009.

Heath, Chip and Heath, Dan. *Made to Stick: Why Some Ideas Survive and Others Die.* Random House, New York, NY, 2008.

Herrmann, Ned. *The Whole Brain Business Book.* McGraw-Hill, New York, NY, 1996.

Hillman, James. From an interview with James Hillman, reprinted with permission of PersonalTransformation.com

Hough, Karen. *The Improvisation Edge: Secrets to Building Trust and Radical Collaboration.* Berrett-Koehler Publishers, Inc., San Francisco, CA, 2011.

House, Chuck and Price, Ray. *The HP Phenomenon.* Stanford University Press, Stanford, CA, 2009.

Khosla, Vinod. "Vinod Khosla's Five-Second Rule." *Fortune,* October 26, 2011.

Krause, Michael and Keltner, Dacher. "Social Class, Contextualism, and Empathic Accuracy." *Psychological Science,* 21 May, 2010.

Limb, Charles J. "Neural Substrates of Spontaneous Musical Performance: An fMRI Study of Jazz Improvisation." *Public Library of Science PLoS One,* February 27, 2008.

Ludeman, Kate and Erlandson, Eddie. *Alpha Male Syndrome.* Harvard Business School Press, Boston, MA, 2006.

Ludeman, Kate and Erlandson, Eddie. "Coaching the Alpha Male." *Harvard Business Review,* May, 2004.

Martin, Joanne and Powers, Melanie. "Truth or Corporate Propaganda: The Value of a Good War Story." *Organizational Symbolism, JAI Press,* 1983.

Mayer, Richard. *Multimedia Learning,* Second Edition. Cambridge University Press, New York, NY, 2009.

Maxwell, Richard. *The Elements of Persuasion.* Harper Collins, New York, NY, 2007.

Meister, Jeanne. "Learning Trends to Watch in 2006." *Chief Learning Officer,* January, 2006.

Mills, C. Wright. *The Power Elite.* Oxford University Press, New York, NY, 2000.

Murthy, N. R. Narayana, "Why Don't We Try To Be India's Most Respected Company?" *Harvard Business Review,* November, 2011.

O'Keefe, Daniel. *Persuasion Theory and Research.* Sage Publications, Thousand Oaks, CA, 2002.

Park, Andrew. "Taming the Alpha Exec." *Fast Company,* May, 2006.

Pentland, Alex. *Honest Signals: How They Shape Our World.* The MIT Press, Cambridge, MA, 2008.

Pfeffer, Jeff. *A Note on Women and Power.* Stanford Business School, December, 2010.

Rauch, Jonathan. "Short Guys Finish Last." *The Economist,* December 23, 1995.

Rogers, Carl. *On Becoming a Person.* Houghton Mifflin, Boston, MA, 1961.

Savage, Adrian. "The Real Glass Ceiling." PNA, Inc., Aptos, CA. www.wipcoaching.com/downloads/the-real-glass-ceiling.pdf

Silverman, Rachel. "Yahoo CEO Carol Bartz: Balance Is a Myth." *Wall Street Journal,* January 15, 2009.

Tufte, Edward R. *The Visual Display of Quantitative Information.* Graphic Press, Cheshire, CN, 2001.

Tzu, Sun. *The Art of War.* Shambhala, Boston, MA, 2002.

.

Endnotes

Introduction
   1. Martin, p. 93

Part I
   1. Tzu, p. xi

Chapter 1
   1. House and Price. p. 220

Chapter 2
   1. O'Keefe. p. 242
   2. Carey. *New York Times* (July 17, 2010)
   3. Beck. *The Wall Street Journal* (September 13, 2011)
   4. Ludeman. *Harvard Business Review* (May, 2004)
   5. Park. *Fast Company* (May, 2006)
   6. Meister. *Chief Learning Officer* (January, 2006)
   7. Coyne and Coyne. *Harvard Business Review* (May, 2007)
   8. House and Price. p. 472
   9. Savage. *The Real Glass Ceiling* (2002)
   10. Ciampa. *Harvard Business Review* (January, 2005)
   11. Krause and Keltner. (May, 2010)
   12. GovernanceMetrics International (June 7, 2010)
   13. Jones. *USA Today* (June 6, 2007)
   14. Davis. (2011)
   15. Rauch. (December 23, 1995)
   16. Jones. *USA Today* (September 4, 2007)

Chapter 8
   1. Hackman (2009)

Chapter 10
   1. Rogers (1961)

Chapter 11
1. Limb (2008)

Chapter 12
1. O'Keefe, p. 244
2. Coyne and Coyne (2007)
3. Right Management, Linkage (2010)
4. Herrmann, Ned (1996) P. 179
5. O'Keefe, p. 221
6. Martin (1983)

Chapter 13
1. Pentland (2008)
2. Mayer (2009)
3. Alley (2003)
4. Tufte (2001)
5. Khosla (2011)

Chapter 15
1. Hillman

Part IV Introduction
1. Cialdini, p. 148

Chapter 15
1. Cosineau, p. 117

Chapter 16
1. Silverman (2009)

Chapter 17
1. Harvard Business School; Working Paper 09-028, 2008

Chapter 18
1. Erikson, p. 266

About the Author

Frederick Gilbert

R ick is the founder and chairman of PowerSpeaking, Inc., a speech communications training company in Redwood City, California. Rick's coaching of more than 200 senior-level executives led to the creation of the award winning *Speaking Up®: Presenting to Executives.*

Before starting his own company, Rick held quality assurance and communications management positions with Hewlett-Packard and Amdahl corporations in Silicon Valley. He is the author or two other books: *PowerSpeaking®: How Ordinary People Can Make Extraordinary Presentations,* and *Jazz, Rock and Roll, and the Revolution in Psychotherapy, 1950–1975* (based on his doctoral dissertation). His articles on communication have appeared in magazines and newspapers nationwide. His PhD from Saybrook University is in humanistic psychology.

www.powerspeaking.com/abouttheauthor